The 70s House

The 70s House

David Heathcote

Photography by **Sue Barr**

Series Designer **Liz Sephton**

contents

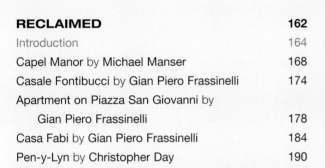

Executive Commissioning Editor: Helen Castle
Development Editor: Mariangela Palazzi-Williams
Design and Editorial Management: Famida Rasheed
Publishing Assistant: Louise Porter

To Bridget and Douglas Barr, Susannah Cox, Fran Hannah, Simon Bradford, Barry Curtis and Jack Heathcote

Acknowledgements

David Heathcote and Sue Barr would like to thank the following for their help with this book: Barbara Neski, Vera Brunner-Kalman, Gian Piero Frassinelli, Alfredo De Vido, Alexandros Tombazis, Sep Marti and family, Mario Campi, Michael Manser CBE, David Johnston OBE, The McCombe family, Christopher Day, Patty Hopkins, Kevin and Alan Tye, Aurora, Costis Sofianos, Mr and Mrs Svolos, Lindy and Paul Manser, Steve Perlbinder and family, Cristian Sabellarosa, Judge Bruce Kaplan, Patricia Grobow, Gerhard Neumann Wolfgang and Gertraude Böttcher, Jan Kleihues and family, The Bianchi family, The Felder family, The Richman family, Richard Henderson, Loring Mandel, Dorothea Strube, Lisa Hockemeyer, Lars Morgenroth, Peter Lang and Charles Jencks.

Michael and Patty Hopkins,
Hopkins House, Hampsteed
London, UK 1975-76

Most of the houses included in this book are lived in by their original owners, many of whom were either the architect or their client; a few were involved in their construction. As in any long-term relationship, the owners of these buildings know their homes in a way that goes far deeper than is possible for any outside observer. They have memory and its evocative triggers where we can only look.

> 'This is what must happen to old married couples, I thought: the young man is preserved in the old one for her, the beauty and grace of the young woman stay fresh in the old one for him.'
>
> Bernhard Schlink, *The Reader*, translated by Carol Brown Janeway, George & Weidenfeld, a division of the Orion Publishing Group, (London), 1998, p107.

Introduction

When Sue Barr and I were researching archive photographs for our book on the Barbican[1] an archivist suggested that we look at Richard Einzig's 1982 book *Classic Modern Houses in Europe*.[2] His glamorous wide-angle pictures of Michael Manser's Capel Manor at Horsmonden, Kent, reminded me of Patrick Gwynne's houses in Blackheath that were equally seemingly drawn by the pen of Ian Fleming. Our interest in individual architect-designed 1970s houses grew from that point as the buildings seemed to share an optimistic freedom lacking in today's ultracontrolled Modernism. We quickly found that apart from Einzig's volume there were almost no books that featured this kind of house produced at the end of that decade. Nor are there many books today that cover any aspect of 1970s architecture except in the most peremptory way as either a codicil to the 1960s or a lull before the 1980s.

The texts that unwittingly set the pattern for this in Britain were Charles Jencks' *Modern Movements in Architecture* of 1973 and *The Language of Post-Modern Architecture* of 1977. The former treated the period up to 1973 as a continuum of the 1960s while the latter created the impression that everything before it was now confined to the end of Modernism and henceforward Post-Modernism would emerge. Jencks' remarks in the conclusion of *The Language of Post-Modern Architecture* were prophetic: 'The next five years promise to be extremely interesting for architects, as the paradigm takes shape – but also probably confused and uncertain.'[3] This was a fatal blow to any consideration of the 1970s because the thing people thought he was talking about emerged in 1980–2. When obviously Post-Modern buildings, like Graves' Portland Public Services Building and Farrell's TV AM, made it easy to understand the new architectural era people simply consigned the 1970s to a 'confused' past.

It should also be remembered that in those days designing houses was not respectable anyway since the underlying assumption, in Britain at least where the largest employer of architects was the country's local authorities,

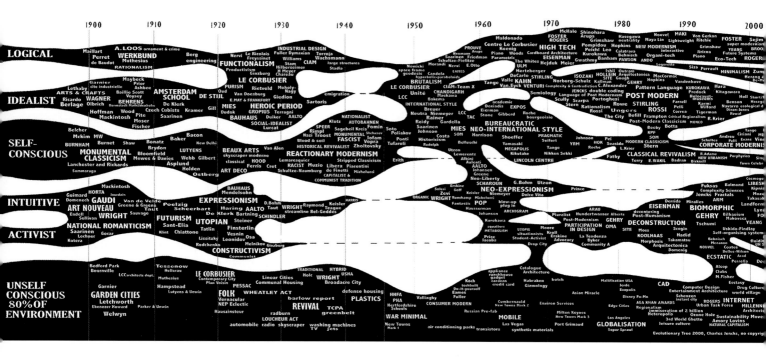

Evolutionary Tree, 1920-1970. The method for determining the six major traditions, from *Modern Movements in Architecture* by Charles Jencks, Penguin Books Ltd (Harmondsworth), 1973, p29.

was that real architecture meant big public projects for government, local authorities, institutions and corporations. A house was nothing then unless it was a social housing project.

So, why might 1970s houses be interesting? At a basic level, since there is plenty published on houses from almost every decade except the 1970s, and because nature abhors a vacuum, these are reasons enough. Houses also represent a relatively pure form of architecture the purposes of which are well understood, and their construction is not as compromised by complexity as other building types. Thus, they are perfect vignettes of architecture and its aesthetics at any given time. Lastly, there are several indicators in the literature, and here Jencks' theorising of 1970s architecture can be allowed to stand, which suggests that the decade was a far richer period for houses than may be supposed from the absence of books about them.

In *Modern Movements in Architecture* there is a famous illustration 'Evolutionary Tree, 1920–1970. The method for determining the six major traditions (movements in architecture).' [4] Leaving aside the details, what is clear from this diagram is that Modern architecture seems to become ever more varied in its divisible manifestations within two main strands between 1950 and 1960. In the 1960s there were even more mini movements or tendencies within a significantly more fragmented whole and this could only continue to increase during the 1970s. The real suggestion of this diagram is that the 1970s might be the most interesting decade for Modern architecture. In the same book the author criticises Modern public architecture but makes no mention of domestic architecture. However, in his later book, *The Language of Post-Modern Architecture*, he seems to suggest that many houses in the 1970s represented some kind of evolutionary shift towards the more literate or rhetorical architecture for which both of these textbooks make a plea.

Thus another reason for a book on 1970s houses is that there are good reasons to suppose that the decade produced some very significant houses in many different modes, and that these pointed the way from the Modern to the Post-Modern. Although this was in fact borne out by our research it turned out to be the least interesting part of it, for what we found as we visited more and more houses was that imposing some teleological order on them was not important because the most significant thing about them is their diversity. Realising this brought to life the dynamic context of 1970s architecture, which for the first time engaged in issues that we now take for granted. These altered the form of houses and the relationships that created them and, as might be expected, the issues and their effects were often contradictory. For instance, while there was an increasingly equal relationship between architect and client, this meant that the client's consumerist needs were more clearly represented in the architecture in the form of more bathrooms and bigger bedrooms and kitchens; and this move away from the earlier primacy of the living area increased the individualism of 1970s domestic design. At the same time a budding Green movement meant that more 'ecological' architecture began to be built but often, paradoxically, as second homes.

There were other more theoretically surprising results from our research, particularly the persistence of the Modernist tradition that conditioned even the new, later seen as anti-Modern Historicism. Historicism emerged in the 1970s not so much as a return to the past but as a way of expanding the possibilities of new architecture. Thus Palladio's work, the Ur-source for Revivalist Historicism in Britain and the USA, was seen and used quite differently in the pre-alpine environment of Ticino, Switzerland, where he was seen almost as part of the local vernacular. In Italy and Switzerland the study of the vernacular that emerged in the 1970s was used to provide new solutions to problems faced by architects that stemmed from increased consumerism in the client and individualism in the architect. Botta's forms bear a clear relation to the local vernacular of sheltering forms but are also a station on the quest for a personal style. Snozzi uses the way that farmers place their buildings as his imprimatur on his Corbusian buildings, while Campi uses Palladian ideas but not forms in his creation of villas that meet the new standards of affluence we all aspire to. Our researches threw up the unexpected conclusion that the most overtly radical of the architects whose work we saw were those who reused old buildings.

Our selection has been as comprehensive as time and money would allow, and we have only shown houses that have appeared in the architectural press or in anthologies of architectural houses that were recognised for their quality or interest at the time they were completed. We have tried to focus our examples in locations that represent clusters of development in the 1970s: northern Italy and Ticino, Athens and its environs, the wealthy suburbs of Berlin and the booming weekender resorts of Long Island. Conversely, in Britain we have tried to look beyond the dynamism of London to other regions that are no less capable of innovation. What these areas all have in common is not so much wealth as ongoing architectural development

By dividing the house into two parts the architect has taken full advantage of a beautiful position overlooking the city of Stuttgart. While one part faces the valley, and is like a bridge over the garden, the other runs parallel to the slope of the site.

There is no rigid form of construction to the house and a wide variety of materials have been used; local sand-stone, rendered brickwork, exposed brick and concrete plus various woods.

The house belongs to a photographer, who intends eventually to build a studio in the grounds.

The house won the Paul Bonatz Prize for architecture in 1960.

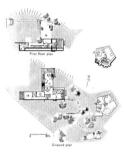

Above: the house from the west, the section on the left is built out from the hillside to take full advantage of the view
Below left and right: the bridged section of the house has a steel frame and is faced in timber
Photos Windstosser

Above: the living area looking towards the external balcony and view beyond. Pine wood is used for the ceiling and elsewhere in this room
Below right: the living-room can be divided to form two smaller sections. Steps lead up to the dining area
Below left: plans
Key: 1 entry 2 hall for exhibiting photographs 3 kitchen 4 utility 5 WC 6 dining 7, 8 living-room 9 balcony 10 open stairs to garden 11 hall 12 child's room 13 bath 14 parent's room 15 covered terrace 16 void under first floor 17, 18 proposed garden studio

First floor plan

Ground plan

in a decade that was marked by serious international economic crises. Many of the houses that we have visited have not been photographed since their original appearance in the press and so the photographs here show them as they are in a mature context after 30 years of occupation. We have tried to avoid the faults of art direction by photographing in natural light conditions and without moving the pictures, furniture or detritus of daily life.

The houses have been arranged in sections that begin with the oldest building and end with the newest. The sections have titles that reflect some obvious correspondences between the houses within the section but these do not correspond to any grand totalising theory. That is not to say that there is no structure, or indeed development, over the course of the book.

The book begins with Modernist and ends with Historicist. The former takes a position that in the 1970s Modernist architecture reassessed itself as a tradition and in some ways looked back to its roots. Historicist looks at the emergence in the 1970s of architecture that sought new inspiration from past concepts more than past building styles. In between we have tried to arrange houses under headings that seem meaningful as different ways of considering groups of buildings from this period. Autoarchitectural, for instance, takes as its premise that there is an aesthetic integrity about a house that an architect builds for himself, since it is as free as possible from

Above and overleaf: *Architectural Design*, 'Small Houses' issues from 1961-62. In the early 1960s there was a remarkable consensus in architecture about the form of the Modern house, which combined low construction, open planning of the living areas and the copious use of full-height glazing to at least one aspect of the living area.

pragmatic compromises. Alternatively, Diffusion says something about the spread of architecture away from a point of origin — about the dissemination of style. The section Reclaimed is about the increased reuse of old buildings which, although not unique to the 1970s, took off in that decade. Independent is there in recognition of the uncommon at the edges of architectural practice, which also seems to have been more common in the 1970s.

If there is a general thesis to the book it is that the 1970s was a period when architects were travelling from their common starting place in the relatively cohesive consensual Modernism of the post-war years up to the late 1960s, but that they didn't have a clear sense of where they were going. This lack of cohesion we take to be a good thing. But to represent a plurality one has to avoid joining up the dots or there emerges an illusory object made real only by the lines drawn between otherwise atomised points. Though there are many conclusions that can be drawn from the houses illustrated in this book it is also possible to ignore them and consider each house individually.

1   David Heathcote, *Barbican: Penthouse Over the City*, photographs by Sue Barr, Wiley-Academy (Chichester), 2004.
2   Richard Einzig, *Classic Modern Houses in Europe*, Nichols Publishing Co. (London), 1982.
3   Charles Jencks, *The Language of Post-Modern Architecture*, Academy Editions (London), 1977, p 101.
4   Charles Jencks, *Modern Movements in Architecture*, Penguin Books Ltd (Harmondsworth), 1973, p 29.

House at Losone, Ticino, Switzerland. Toward the end of the 1960s there began to be some breakdown in the dominance of the open-plan formula with its combination of large glazed areas and living/dining/cooking areas. The Andina House at Losone shows the Ticinese interest in the work of Louis Kahn on the exterior and inside there is an absolute separation between the kitchen, and the living and dining rooms, which are arranged around an atrium light well. However, this is an unusual example of a bit of an architectural cul-de-sac and the dominance of Modernist room layouts remained well into the 1970s

House in Houston, Texas

Howard Barnstone & Partners

Above: the south front of the house. The double volume living-room occupies the two bays on the right

Below: the entrance on the north side

Photos Fred Winchell

Below right: plans
Key: **1** *dining area* **2** *living area* **3** *breakfast room* **4** *garage* **5** *laundry* **6** *kitchen* **7** *entry* **8** *patio* **9** *study* **10** *bathroom* **11** *dressing room* **12** *bedroom* **13** *upper section of living area* **14** *housekeeper*

The house is in a prosperous suburb of large homes, well-tended lawns and many trees. The site is quite flat.

The structure is a simple steel frame set on a concrete slab, the five bays filled with glass or pink brick panels, the steel being left exposed and painted white. Glass walls are recessed behind the frame to give more solar protection, but service areas, bathrooms, etc., being artificially ventilated are pushed to the face of the frame.

The house is planned on a 4ft. module; it is fitted with year-round air conditioning.

151 Architectural Design March 1962

First floor plan

Ground floor plan

Above: the living-room looking towards the study alcove at left and the entrance hall at right

Below left: the double volume living-room with recessed glass wall facing south

Below right: detail of the fitted kitchen, which adjoins the breakfast room and a small patio on the east side of the house

152

MODERNIST

In any discussion of 20th-century domestic architecture there needs to be some distinction between modern living and Modernism. Modernism in architecture was a reaction to modern living that sought both to respond to and prognosticate about the best ways that architecture could deal with the rapidly changing world of the 20th century.

These changes were many and varied according to geographic and social context but, relativism aside, the main changes that affected privately owned domestic architecture in northern Europe and America were: families became smaller; households with servants and public functions (like country houses) virtually ceased to exist; affluence and leisure among the moderately wealthy increased; and motorised personal transport became ubiquitous, as did technologies for domestic comfort, communication and entertainment.

Modernist

The response of Modernist architects in respect of middle- and upper-income housing was to develop houses that were smaller, accommodated the altered sociology of the family, and were equipped with the appropriate domestic technology as it became easily available. Architects also reconsidered the materials suitable for domestic design in general tending to appropriate materials from industrial building and adapt them to domestic settings. Perhaps the most important revision in architects' thinking in response to new patterns of living in the 20th century was to develop new spaces appropriate to contemporary life. Increasingly, as the century progressed open-planned living areas became a consistent feature of the modern home. Open planning referred to the joining of the formerly separate rooms used for cooking, eating and relaxing into one large living space. In Britain by the late 1950s open planning was a sufficiently consensual design feature to become introduced into speculatively built homes, though it had earlier been a feature of public housing for reasons of economy as much as any other more benign consideration. It was only in the 1970s, after the long period of international architectural consensus about the nature of the modern home that had emerged in the 1940s, that architects began fundamentally to rethink the design of houses in response to new conditions of modern life.

The Modernist consensus about the design of houses, which was almost worldwide in the early 1960s, was based on a very simple formula that had its origins in the pioneering Modernism of the early 20th century; particularly the work of Le Corbusier, Frank Lloyd Wright and Mies van der Rohe. These architects worked on projects for modest houses as well as luxurious villas. This combination of experience led to the application to smaller houses of certain spatial and experiential qualities that had evolved for more luxurious projects. The most significant development they shared was the recognition that space and light define affluence, and this idea was itself based on one –

well established by the time of the Arts and Crafts movement – that light and air are beneficial to health. Thus, the more space and light that could surround day-to-day living the better life would be. In a small home this would mean that activities like washing and sleeping would have to take place in relatively smaller spaces in order to provide a larger living space.

These architects, who were by no means the only ones pursuing these ideas about space planning, were also aware of the luxurious pleasures of modern life, such as cars and reliable bathrooms, as well as those of the previous century, like the dressing room and dramatic spaces for entertaining, and they designed buildings that combined luxury and affluence in some aspects and a more functional, compensational use of space in others.

In some fundamental respects their attitudes to architecture differed, particularly with respect to space and nature. Le Corbusier brought an almost *ancien régime* formality to his conception of domestic space, and at the top of the spatial hierarchy was the classical double-height space, which was present in his large villas like Villa Roche (1924) as well as the small Pavilion de l'Esprit Nouveau (1925). Wright, on the other hand, in general preferred the large, low, open space with its timeless and classless intimacy and this is most spectacularly evident in his house Falling Water for Kaufmann at Bear Run, Pennsylvania (1935–8). Mies van der Rohe used a very similar formulation of living space in his Tugendhat House at Brno in Czechoslovakia (1930), which also featured large curtain windows that, in a manner similar to Wright's designs for Falling Water, integrated interior and exterior space. The attitude of these architects with regard to the position of houses in relationship to the land differed. Wright's most influential houses hugged the land as at Taliesin West (1937) as opposed to Le Corbusier's, which stood above it, while Mies van der Rohe, who in the end may have been the most influential in this respect, occupied a median position, as seen at the Farnsworth House (1946-50). There the house sits separated from the land but is sufficiently near to the ground for viewers to feel that they are in a natural viewpoint vis-à-vis the landscape.

In the post-war years of European reconstruction the pioneering work of the pre-war Modernist architects stood as an exemplar to the new generations of the late 1940s, 1950s and early 1960s. In the design of individual houses Le Corbusier's pre-war villas and his 1956 Maisons Jaoul exerted a general influence, as did Wright's Usonian houses (1938). However, it was American houses such as Mies van der Rohe's Farnsworth House or his Chamberlain House designed with Walter Gropius (1940), and houses like Falling Water and another Kaufmann house at Palm Springs by the Austrian émigré Neutra (1946), that were far more influential on the form of post-war architect-designed homes. All were essentially bungalows with open living areas surrounded by curtain windows.

The new generations of architects were aware of these houses and their plans through their dissemination in the newly vital architectural magazines. These forced domestic Modernism to develop at a fast pace in the post-war period, helped by reconstruction and the economic boom.

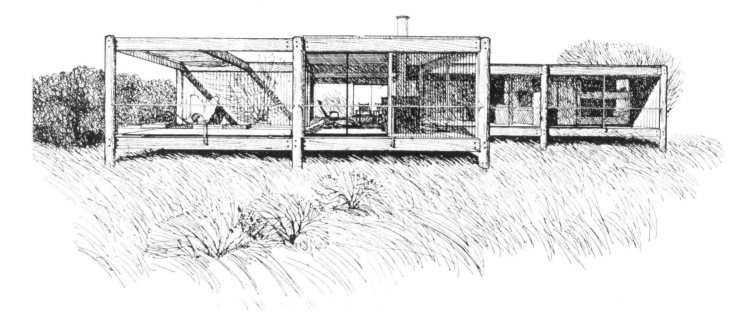

There was almost as much interest in new American house design(s) among speculative house builders in post-war Europe as there was in the USA, because they represented new standards in interior specification and yet were far more prefabricated than European buildings. The European designs were very often for bungalows, and as late as 1967 the British speculative house builder Taylor Woodrow offered the 'Californian' open-planned house — its name a recognition of the popular idea of the origin of the style.

By the early 1960s there seems to have been a widespread consensus among architects about the form of the Modern home, which was based on American precedents from the late 1930s and early 1940s. The archetypal, modern, architect-designed home from the late 1940s through to the late 1960s could be characterised as a detached single-storey building with an 'L' form (giving a double aspect) set on a rise or above the land around it. Inside, the majority of the available space would be given over to some form of open-planned living area while bedrooms and bathrooms took a secondary role. This is not to say that there were no other forms of houses built by architects, rather that the forms the profession selected as exemplars of contemporary international practice in publications like *Architectural Design*'s annual 'New Houses' issues were most usually of this type.

Part of the success of this type of house lay in the architectural ethos of post-war Modernism that regarded the architect's role not as a stylist but, quite the reverse, as a non-stylist who sought to develop ever better means of creating domestic environments, but through materials and technologies rather than forms. This attitude encouraged the refinement of form rather than

Julian Neski, drawing of the Neski weekend House, Watermill, Long Island, 1965. Julian Neski (1927-2004) has been credited with drawing every detail on the projects undertaken by Neski Associates. His regard for detail is evident in these presentation drawings of projects in context. This level of attention to detail represents a key element in the Modernist architect's approach to the craft of architecture, where the ownership of design comes as much from the origination of the details as from the overall vision.

constant attempts to find new forms. This 'functionalist' approach to design in the architectural profession was a fundamental criticism of Jencks' critiques of contemporary architecture in both his *Modern Movements in Architecture* and *The Language of Post-Modernism* as he saw this astylar approach as a fundamental denial of the architect's role as a form giver.

The popularity of the single-storey, open-plan house remained into the 1970s, for example Michael Manser's Miesian glass box at Horsmonden (1970) and the Rogers and Design Research Unit house at Wimbledon (1972–3). However, by the early 1970s this consensus about the form of domestic architecture was beginning to erode among architects, though it had reached its zenith in middle-income speculative building.

From the mid-1960s there had been a critical reassessment of Modernism in the work of Venturi, Rossi and Banham among others, and this reflected a mood of introspection in architecture that continued and became more critical during the 1970s culminating in a widespread rejection of Modernism. However, this must be seen against a general cultural nostalgia in Europe and America that, although reflecting a dislike of the present, also displayed a great enthusiasm for early Modernism. As late as 1979 the Hayward Gallery had a large retrospective called 'Thirties: British Art and Design Before the War', which enjoyed huge popular success. In the early 1970s, despite critiques of modern architecture, there seems to have been a positive

Julian Neski, drawing of Batten House, East Hampton, Long Island, 1972.

reappraisal of the early years of International Modernism and of Le Corbusier, in particular, as a result of the publication in the late 1960s and early 1970s of many books reassessing his work following his death in 1965, for example that of Boesiger and Girsberger, which was published in 1967.[1] Luigi Snozzi, architect of the Casa Kalmann, speaking in 1986, represents both the attitudes of the post-war Modernist architect and the modified attitude of one who has reconsidered Modernism in the light of later 1960s and 1970s critiques: 'The Modern Movement, seen in a critical context, represents a crucial reference point for my work, and the great emotional response that certain buildings have elicited – and still elicit – in me have certainly influenced my mode of expression. Rather than searching for a style I am concerned with a search for a formal reduction: against the loud formal din of Post-Modernism I propose highly restrained silence.'[2]

In reconsidering Le Corbusier there was a return to his villa forms of the 1920s with their combination of aristocratic formality (double-height spaces, grand entries to spaces) and 'machine aesthetic' (utilitarian industrial finishes and technological fittings). Equally apparent in the new Modernist homes of the 1970s was a tendency to make them stand proud of the land, to become Corbusian villas rather than Miesian houses, by designing them as taller and more complicated geometric forms, which gave them a sculptural abstract quality that was lacking in the old land-hugging, single-storey form.

Snozzi's houses, such as the Casa Kalmann (1974–5) and the nearby Casa Bianchetti 1975–7, show a clear relation to the work of Le Corbusier in the 1920s, both in their use of spaces (double-height living areas and mezzanines) and materials (smooth white concrete and slim metal-framed fenestration).

The clients who commissioned houses in the 1970s also had different ideas, not so much about style – although Judge Kaplan echoed Snozzi's remarks when he said of his house by the Neskis that it was less dominant of the owner than a house by Norman Jaffe (see Perlbinder House, p214) – but more about domestic design, and they seem to have indicated some return to an earlier formality as well as a greater appreciation of what earlier Modernists regarded as 'human functions', such as cooking and bathing. Thus, some of the Modernist houses of the 1970s included more and larger bathrooms in more complex 'master suites' and began to include larger kitchens and dining areas. For example, Loring Mandel, having seen the small kitchen designed by Charles Gwathmey for his mother's house at Amagansett (1965), specified a much larger kitchen for his own house (now the Richman House) as he and his wife enjoyed cooking. Equally the Neski's Grobow House has a very splendid his and hers dressing room–bathroom that recalls Le Corbusier's remark that one should never sleep and dress in the same room.

Although most of the examples in this section have been chosen to represent houses that are based on a reassessment of International Modernism, and Le Corbusier in particular, there was a continuation throughout the 1970s of the later Miesian Modernist aesthetic in homes like the Manser and Rogers' houses. In the mid-1970s this style evolved, not least through the efforts of Rogers and Piano at the Centre Georges Pompidou, into an almost Mannerist off-the-shelf Industrial Modernism, or Adhocism as Jencks terms it. This is evident in the Hopkins House (1975–6), which eschews the old, heavy-industry materials and forms of Le Corbusier in favour of an etiolated, metallic, solid-state lightness in the form of two Miesian modular glass boxes.

The Modernist architecture of the 1970s was more self-conscious than that of the previous generation. This may be because the profession was in general beginning to reassess its position by re-examining its antecedents and considering areas of architectural design that had been neglected, with the purpose of escaping the orthodoxy that Modernist architecture had become. This general re-examination of architecture led to a self-conscious pursuit of hybridisation in architecture so that it is possible that a Corbusian Modernist house of the 1970s could also adopt elements of newly reconsidered vernacular practice or renaissance practice as is the case with Snozzi's Casa Kalmann. However, where this was the case, these references were subsumed into a Modernist whole and remain implicit whereas later practice, which began to emerge later in the 1970s, was to make these features much more explicit.

1   Willy Boesiger and Hans Girsberger (Eds), *Le Corbusier 1910–1965*, Thames and Hudson (London), 1967.
2   Luigi Snozzi, 'Notes of a design process' in *Urban Renewal at Monte Carasso*, 9H Gallery (London), 1986, p 5. Quoted in Gerardo Brown-Manrique*, The Ticino Guide*, Princeton Architectural Press (Princeton), 1989, p 19.

Kaplan House

Barbara and Julian Neski
Sagaponack, Long Island, New York, USA   1970

For many the attraction of Long Island lies in the south fork of the eastern end of it and a group of historic villages known as the Hamptons. These could, if they were on a smaller scale, be located in East Anglia with their tastefully semi-matt-painted clapboard houses lining tidy streets, and greens punctuated by churches and the occasional windmill. Of course, English village streets aren't lined with tobacconist-sized branches of Tiffany and Chanel and nor do their side roads lead to hedged suburbs of Gatsby mansions. The real draw of the Hamptons for the settlers of the 1960s and 1970s was the crystalline light on the long, duned, sandy beaches facing the Atlantic swell. These new generations of Long Island residents sought out more isolated sites, which became available as the local farmers began to sell off plots at the edges of their land.

Between Bridgehampton and East Hampton, with Amagansett the epicentre of Hampton society, lies Sagaponack. Its long, straight beach is reached from the Montauk Highway down Main Street, which runs for almost all the few miles of its length between fields except when it passes through the tiny hamlet of Sagaponack with the veranda of its post office facing a small green. Though remote by the standards of the Hamptons, down by the ocean the ubiquitous loop roads and cul-de-sacs of plotland development have began to erode the wildness of the country. Back in 1970, though, the Kaplan House was the master of all it surveyed from its position behind the dunes, safe from the scouring currents that erode Long Island's coastline at this point.

The style on Long Island at the time was divided between the abstract New York Five approach of pure geometry and a more European style of Modernism that had its roots in Le Corbusier's villas of the 1920s. The Neskis, who had both worked for Breuer in his New York office before starting their own practice, worked in both styles.[1] Their Simon House at Remsenburg (1972), also on Long Island, an *Architectural Record* House of 1973, was an essay in the New York style, being cubic in form and rising through 11 levels in 30 feet with openings placed to favour special views. The Kaplan House is a purely Corbusian design, owing a lot to the Villa Savoye. The strange quality of the Long Island Modernist houses is that whatever their European counterparts achieve with concrete is here undertaken utilising the local balloon frame and cedar siding construction method. A significant architectural advantage of wooden Modernism is its structural simplicity and sculptural possibilities. This means that whatever can be drawn can be easily achieved, almost with a hammer, a saw and some staples. That said, to

Above: **Kaplan House, Long Island, USA.** When the house was built it commanded uninterrupted views and this was reflected in the outward-looking design. Over the years the land around the house near the roads has been sold off and developed. There is little control over building in the Hamptons, as can be seen from the various structures that punctuate the land to the rear of the house.

Right: **Kaplan House, Long Island, USA.** There are three ways into the house, all of which converge on a corner of the building. The large void on the ground level indicates the garage–store, which has an internal door to the house, and next to this entrance is the front door to the house that accesses the internal stairs. The relative position of these is indicated by the curved section on the top floor above the corner of the house. The third way into the house, a good party entrance, is the ramp leading up from the front door and garage to the wide balcony on the first floor. With its wide-open spaces inside and out, which can be joined by opening up the windows, this floor forms the public space that is such an important element in Long Island weekend houses. Above are the private rooms of the owner and a smaller balcony with better views.

Kaplan House, Long Island, USA. A free-standing chimney, the fire traditionally facing the sitting area, divides the living from the dining area. A breakfast bar, itself an archetype of Modernist internal planning, lying at the elbow of the L, indicates the separation of the kitchen area from the living and dining areas. Another feature of Modernist internal planning is the dislike of central, or indeed any, intrusive type of lighting. Here, lights are recessed into the ceiling. An earlier incarnation of this minimalist approach to lighting was tracklights.

achieve the smooth skin demanded by Modernist forms and the weatherproofing demanded by the climate requires craft. At the Kaplan House the cedar siding was left to weather to grey and is attached on the diagonal on the exterior, which imbues the structure with a sense of dynamism.

Unlike the Villa Savoye the Kaplan House has a view and this is celebrated in every aspect of the structure. Though built on three floors, the house is mainly articulated through the upper two levels with the ground level functioning as a kind of podium, though it is replete with bedrooms giving onto inset verandas, a bathroom and a storeroom by the front door.

The upper storeys are divided into a piano nobile and an upper, smaller floor. It is from these floors that an almost 360-degree view of the ocean and Sagaponack Lake can be seen. From a distance the house appears as an eroded cube. The ground floor is solid square with a couple of voids inserted for verandas and windows. The middle floor, though square in outline, is clearly mainly a facade opening onto a deep balcony that runs three-quarters of the perimeter of the building. Sited above the void of the front entrance below and the Corbusian ramp rising to the first-floor balcony, is the main body of the first floor. Accessed by a top-lit spiral stair running the full height of the house, it is one large kitchen–living–dining area. It has full-height,

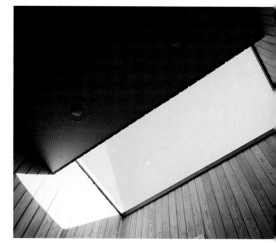

Left and below: **Kaplan House, Long Island, USA.** Another bugbear of Modernist house design was stairs and the most common solutions were to create sculptural effects, introduce dramatic lighting, and minimalise the volume of the stairs by using open treads and as few structural elements as possible. The most effective type for these principles is the spiral stair set in a top-lit shaft. Here care has been paid to reducing the handrail to a minimum using steel and similarly reducing the profile of the whole staircase by using white treads, thus splitting the volume into two parts. Equally, the light in the well is maximised by the use of a very large skylight, reducing apparent volume still further through strong bright lighting.

opening windows facing the deep veranda and the ocean from the living–dining side of the long L of the plan, while the kitchen in the short side has its work surfaces facing the view inland through half-height windows. The kitchen is separated from the dining area by a long run of cupboards with a worktop, and the dining area is separated from the living area by a freestanding chimney breast. The first floor is capable of holding about 150 guests. Upstairs the master bedroom and bathroom suite has its own roof terrace and the otherwise smaller square exterior is made sculptural by the appearance of the circular stairwell.

Some features of the design pick up on ideas that the Neskis used in their more geometric New York-style houses. The huge skylight casting sunlight down the full height of the interior is one, as is the circular form of the stairwell being used as an external decorative feature, and the use of a long access way. Here it is a Corbusian ramp, while at the Simon House it is a bridge and at the Gorman House at Amagansett it is a simple raised wooden path across the sand. Another feature taken from the Gorman House is the external shower room, here as much for the swimming pool as for the sea just over the dunes. But while the New York style suited the packed dunes of Amagansett and the wooded site of the Simon House at Remsenburg, the Corbusian Modernism of the Neskis was very well suited to the open sites of Sagaponack and, inland at Watermill, the setting of the Grobow House.

1   Breuer had emigrated to the USA in 1937. He first worked with Gropius and also taught with him, training among others Johnson and Rudolph.

Right: **Gorman House, Long Island, USA.**
A recurrent feature in Neski designs was the use of long access paths as sculptural elements. Here, at his earlier Gormann House, the path across the sand functions like a bridge increasing the apparent footprint of the house and defining the border between public and private space. At the Kaplan House *(below)* the Corbusian ramp performs the same function of psychological enlargement by making this entry to the grand public areas of the house as long and as public as possible.

Above: **Kaplan House, Long Island, USA.** The external shower is a subtle but definite statement of the restricted function of the house. In its spartan affluence it is emblematic of the beach-house aesthetic and of a particular class of people. Modernism has in many ways the same connotations; it is the architecture of the healthy tan.

Grobow House

Barbara and Julian Neski
Watermill, Long Island, New York, USA   1972

The Kaplan House, though Modernist and Corbusian, proclaims its beach status through its weathered cedar exterior, which resembles a clinker-built fishing boat in comparison to the smooth, white, ocean liner-like appearance of the Grobow House.

The setting of the Grobow House was originally in spectacularly open farmland right on the western edge of the Hamptons, between Watermill and the huge Atlantic Golf Club. The house was designed to stand freely as a white monument in a green sea looking towards Mill Pond across the unhedged fields. Over time, though, it has been surrounded by newer developments, and it is a measure of the quality of the design that it has been able to adapt to its more enclosed surroundings chiefly through the current owner's development of an English Edwardian-style garden.

The original house takes the form of a two-storey double square but it has now been extended via a glass lobby to join a new accommodation block in a similar style, though more square in form, with garages and a study below and bedrooms above. The principal facade of the southern block is glazed to the full two-storey height for its entire length though this is inset like a mirror in a frame allowing a balcony that runs for just over half the length of the facade within the perimeter of the building. All the exterior surfaces are made from plywood sheet sidings to allow for a smooth finish and the whole building, including the window frames, is painted white against which the inset windows appear black.

The house is entered from the rear via a large single-storey glazed lobby, which gives onto two studies, left and right, while to the front it enters the kitchen–dining–living area at its midpoint. The hall also contains a large, complicated stairwell. Here a very Corbusian, narrow, spiral stair with waist-height, solid banister walls topped by a black iron rail leads up to a hall area lit from the north by a large square window. The guest bedrooms and the dressing room for the master bedroom at the back of the house are accessed via a long, narrow 'bridge' that continues the design of the stairs and forces one to turn three times in order to reach these rooms at the rear.

Downstairs the spaces are far less complex, with a square, double-height living room to one side and a single-height dining room–kitchen to the other side. The entire southern wall of this room is glazed to its full height while the short wall of the living area has an open fireplace. The dining area faces the view while to the rear is a large galley-style kitchen separated off by a work surface and cupboards that run the length of the division between the two areas. There are no curtains, the walls are white and the floor is black slate.

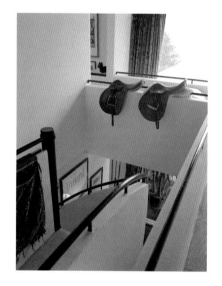

Grobow House, Long Island, USA. The staircase, landing and stairwell are made into a complex and interesting space by the separation of the stairs and landing from the stairwell. The narrowness of the stairs and landing, and the treatment of the banisters, recall Le Corbusier's designs of entrance halls in the 1930s and the stairs of the 1950s. Here, they minimise the footprint of the stairs below and maximise light levels on both floors.

Upstairs the master bedroom originally ran half the length of the main facade
and opened through full-height windows onto an enclosed balcony. Later the
Neskis divided this space into a smaller master bedroom and another small
bedroom, and extended the division out onto the balcony to maintain the
privacy of the two rooms. To the rear of the upper floor, over the bridge, lies
a particularly Neski, and very un-Corbusian, feature – a 'superluxe' dressing
room. Facing the rear facade is a long, low window above which are mirrored
cupboards while below there are built-in drawers with inset his and hers oval
handbasins set in at each end of a white, timber-edged melamine surface.
Behind this runs a narrow galley access and on the inner side of this there is
a bathroom at one end. The rest of the space is taken up by walk-in
cupboards accessed by a short passage running at 90 degrees to the main
run down the room. This short run leads back to a built-in chest of drawers in
melamine, above which is a built-in mirror, all below a skylight. On each side
of the corridor are sliding doors giving entry to the two walk-in wardrobes.

Despite its Corbusianism the Grobow House represents an emergent new
trend in house design. As well as having the by now conventional double-
height, fully glazed, log-fired living space and combined open-plan
dining–kitchen area, the Grobow House is among the first Modernist houses
to provide sleeping–bathing and, here, dressing facilities that match the
leisured luxury of the living spaces. Where the Kaplan House is designed for
entertaining the Grobow House has the feel of a very private retreat for a
couple who, though seeking seclusion, demand urban standards of luxury.
The Neskis provided this in a manner that was quite alien to earlier Modernist
architectural designs, which had long created living space by sacrificing all
other spaces.

Above: Grobow House, Long Island, USA.
These pictures show the complexity of use and formal simplicity of open planning. The open-planned principal space of the Grobow House follows the Corbusian pattern seen in his Unité d'Habitation (1947) of a double-height space with a single-height space to the rear. That being said, this layout was so conventional by the 1970s that it had become simply Modernist rather than purely Corbusian. Here, the windows run the length of both spaces, unifying them and removing the front and back feeling of Le Corbusier's original design.

Right: Grobow House, Long Island, USA. It is conventional today to imagine that Modernist spaces can only be minimally filled, with light and transparent furniture. This convention is really the effect of the revivalist dogma of Modernism now. This interior with its traditional furnishings shows that the purpose of open planning was to break down the formality of traditional European room hierarchies rather than control how people filled space. It is the plentiful light, absence of walls and the seamless transition from fireside to dinner table that is Modernist rather than how the space is, or is not, filled.

Grobow House, Long Island, USA. Many
Modernist house plans treat all but the living areas
as service rooms and their size is often reduced to
maximise the space available for open planning.
By the 1970s there was a growing demand for
more luxurious designs for bedrooms and bathrooms that reflected increasing materialism and
affluence. Here the architects have re-created the
sort of dressing room that was more common
in the pre-Modernist designs of country house
architects before the First World War. Since the
1970s it has become the number of bathrooms
and their size, rather than the provision of dressing
rooms, that has defined the status of a house as
the dress codes of leisure become less important
than the cult of the body.

Richman House

Richard Henderson

Huntington Bay, Long Island, New York, USA   1972

This house was commissioned from the firm of Gwathmey Henderson and was designed by Richard Henderson around 1970. The client, Loring Mandel, had been searching for an architect to build a house on a 2-acre site that he owned covering a small valley in an old 60-acre arboretum, and found that he couldn't afford the likes of Meier but could afford Gwathmey Henderson. The site lies on the north shore of Long Island not far from Long Island Sound in the midst of the wealthy, long-established, Home Counties-type suburb of Huntington Bay. This area has none of the open vistas of the Hamptons but consists of heavily wooded and hilly terrain with a sandy soil. It is within commuting distance of Manhattan, where the new owners used to live before they had their first child. It is a self-consciously plutocratic environment of country clubs, beach clubs and well-tended and secured desirable 'estates', very different to the Bohemian, trendy East End of 1970–2. Even now Henderson's design is unusual in an area of large, early 20th-century residences and POMO 'Macmansions'.

Thanks to an article by Loring Mandel in the *New York Times* of 6 December 1970 we know what he wanted from his architect: 'The house would not be a jewel in a setting. The valley was the jewel, and the house had to be fashioned to let us see it in bloom or in snow.' In fact, it is not so much the valley itself that is the jewel but the planting of azaleas and rhododendrons beneath tall trees in the setting of a natural amphitheatre, which is still the case. The setting of the house, along the contour of one side of the valley and looking down and across a wide lawn to a wall of exotic shrubs and fine trees, takes the building out of the present and into a setting of Late Victorian splendour.

The design of the house is unusual in combining three styles of architecture that are related but separate strands of Modernism. The wish of the client that the house must respect and serve the site meant that the architect drew upon the long American Modernist tradition of tying the building into the site and creating a place for the contemplation of nature. In contrast to this, the form of the architecture and its plan combine the new styles of architecture of which Gwathmey Henderson were pioneers – the formal geometries of the New York Five School and the pre-war European Modernism of vaguely nautical white walls, balconies, pilotis and thick, flat roofs. Unusually, the building also combines a concrete and wooden structure that adds to the sense of a hybrid Modernism expertly synthesised. The

Richman House, Long Island, USA. The house seen from the entrance has the abstract geometry of the New York architectural fashion of the day, but the garden facade is a more complex synthesis of the American Modernist regard for linking a building to its landscape and pre-war European Deco Modernism in its use of continuous forms for the balcony and roofline. There is a nostalgic feel to the house, and its siting in an older, grander and more man-made landscape than was usual for Modernist villas may reflect the cultural nostalgia that made the film *The Great Gatsby* such a hit in the early 1970s.

Above: Richman House, Long Island, USA.
The original client's interest in cooking resulted in custom-built cooking and preparation areas with built-in fittings. This was the most advanced practice of the time, signifying efficiency, ergonomics and hygiene all in one go. What designs like these did not take into account was the emerging dynamic of consumerism, which has resulted in the regular and complete refitting of kitchens and bathrooms every few years.

Opposite: Richman House, Long Island, USA.
The kitchen is large and bright, with a dining table-sized breakfast bar clearly indicating the room's importance in the house. The original client enjoyed cooking and made a point of specifying the type of large family kitchen that is standard nowadays. When the house was designed it was more usual for architects to specify small galley kitchens linked to open-planned living areas.

experience of the building takes the viewer through these three modes, which modulate the mood of the house from urban to leisured to proprietorial pride, as any suburban house should.

The approach to the house is down a steep, short drive that leads to a car-turning area in front of the house. The first view of the building is of a blank, pale-grey wooden container with a grey garage door inset that leads to a double-height glazed tower via a wide path between the long side of the container and the concrete retaining wall of the hillside. Towards the tower on the left is a wide, glazed front door. This initial impression follows the language seen elsewhere on Long Island (in part initiated by the house of Gwathmey's mother at Amagansett) of strict geometry and unpredictable openings, a typology with a conceptual urban feel – a sculpture on the land rather than in it. The upper floor houses the kitchen and living areas while downstairs are bedrooms, bathrooms, a dressing room, a playroom and a study. It is possible to enter the house via either of two glazed entrances, but while the second is what one sees the first is what one enters and this leads into a tight little hall and also a WC, which is reached via a small utility room. This constriction prepares the visitor for the next experience of open space.

Turning through 90 degrees the view goes down the length of the house to the fireplace via the kitchen and living room. The freestanding chimney breast is surrounded by straight transparent walls leading out to a semicircular balcony with views into the woods. This sudden vista of the whole house from a cramped entrance is a *coup de théâtre* and emphasises the sense of release at arriving home. The effect is increased by the contrast of the dark entrance hall and the much lighter kitchen, an effect magnified by a circular skylight immediately above the entrance from the hall to the kitchen. Coming first into the kitchen is no less pleasurably domestic after a bad journey from Manhattan.

The kitchen, with a built-in breakfast bar, is interesting for two reasons. First, it is treated as a room in itself and given full-length windows onto the garden. Second, it is large and beautifully fitted along one wall leaving a great deal of circulation space. This is a new type of kitchen, which recognises the pleasure of cooking and eating, and not the more common 'galley' of the period. Mr Mandel was a keen cook and had made a point of specifying a large kitchen after seeing the small kitchen that Gwathmey had put in his mother's house at Amagansett. The square living–dining room beyond is fully glazed on the two sides facing the garden, and is back-lit from the side furthest from the garden by the double-height glazing of the second entrance

Richman House, Long Island, USA. The Richman House has an interesting division of space within the restricted number of rooms (two) on the main floor. Unusually for a Modernist house the kitchen is separate from the open-plan living–dining room. Also unusual is the fact that there are two front entrances, one through the kitchen the other directly into the living area. The reason for this is that guests can arrive and be entertained without any awareness of the kitchen while at other times the owners can enter directly into the heart of the home.

and stairwell, which is itself top-lit by an upper clerestory reflected into the house via a curved wooden wall. This second entrance is a theatrical device through which guests may enter, thus coming directly into the most dramatic space and avoiding the kitchen. The views from these upper rooms look across the valley to the shrubbery and, no matter which entrance is used, one is immediately struck by the panoramic view.

Downstairs are the private spaces of bedrooms. Two for children, with their own bathroom and playroom, each looking out through full-height windows across a joint patio sheltered by the balcony above. The far end of the lower floor, which corresponds to the end of the living space above, forms the master suite and the patio of this space is screened from that of the other bedrooms. A large bedroom with an open fire and full-height glazing to the patio leads onto a writing study that follows the arc of the balcony above and is lit on the garden side by a picture window. To the rear of the master bedroom and the study are a dressing room and a bathroom, the whole ensemble forming a distinct suite. The vast glazed areas of the house are made possible by the use of discreet cross walls in the lower storey and pilotis on both floors; and because the building is wooden, with the exception of the floors and retaining walls, the structural supports can be slighter than one instinctively expects, which adds to the sense of open space.

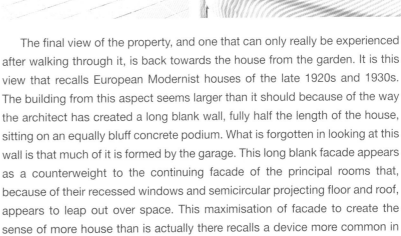

Right and below: Richman House, Long Island, USA. The house combines the circle and the square and, although the plan combines only one circle with an inner square, the combination of the two forms is present in all the spaces of the house without disrupting the practicality of regular-shaped rooms – with the exception of the writing study, where a curved wall makes it difficult to stare out of the window. This simple contrast of geometric forms may reflect some Vitruvian contrast of nature and civilisation, but it is more probably representative of the Modernist architects' self-proclaimed role as sculptural form-givers, that is so evident in the architecture of Long Island in the 1970s.

Opposite: Richman House, Long Island, USA. An archetypal Modernist living space – a fireside with a panoramic view. This combination of the comforts of home and the illusion of boundless space was a much sought after sensation in American Modernist design as it epitomised a key part of American national identity in both the romantici-sation of big nature and the use of technology to tame it.

The final view of the property, and one that can only really be experienced after walking through it, is back towards the house from the garden. It is this view that recalls European Modernist houses of the late 1920s and 1930s. The building from this aspect seems larger than it should because of the way the architect has created a long blank wall, fully half the length of the house, sitting on an equally bluff concrete podium. What is forgotten in looking at this wall is that much of it is formed by the garage. This long blank facade appears as a counterweight to the continuing facade of the principal rooms that, because of their recessed windows and semicircular projecting floor and roof, appears to leap out over space. This maximisation of facade to create the sense of more house than is actually there recalls a device more common in the late 19th- and early 20th-century houses that are dotted among the surrounding wooded enclaves.

Casa Kalman

Luigi Snozzi

Brione Sopra Minusio, Locarno, Ticino, Switzerland   1975

The Casa Kalman stands on an improbable site in the middle of a hairpin bend on the outskirts of a village above Lake Maggiore. The site is so steep and narrow that the architect, Luigi Snozzi, was at first reluctant to work on the project. His solution, however, turns the problem of the site to an advantage by creating an architectural environment that combines interior with exterior, an overt Modernism with an equally overt Classicism.

The owners of the house, a left-wing family originally from Hungary, sought out Snozzi because of his politics, and one result of this is that the quality of the house comes from the excellence of the architecture and not from any other luxurious features. It is usual to talk of house and garden but the Casa Kalman is really both at the same time. The 'house' part of the building is a Corbusian villa with a strong debt to the Pavilion de l'Esprit Nouveau. The interior space has a very simple layout. The platform of the main body of the house is buried in the hill on one side while on the other it towers above the road. The interior of this space is given over to two features – a service basement and the entrance to the house. This entrance is the first hint of Historicism in the villa as, in the manner of a Florentine Renaissance palazzo, a small lobby leads straight to a long terracotta staircase and thereby the first floor. This simple device creates a sense of drama, scale and expectation in what is a small house.

In fact, Snozzi designed the house in the Renaissance manner as a series of transits and vistas, and in this sense the stairs are a transition from a long, dimly lit space into a large, light and unrestricted space. This is the main living area, which combines a double-height space, a fully glazed wall looking onto a long but terminated vista and, on the reverse wall, a large open fireplace all in a firmly Corbusian language of white walls and steel-framed fenestration. Behind the fireplace is a kitchen–dining area of an elegantly utilitarian nature; the owners remarked that when the architect asked what kind of fittings were required they asked for good basic quality with no other conditions. Up further stairs are two bedrooms of which one is simple and almost styleless while the main room is in the form of a mezzanine above the living area, again Corbusian, opening through a fully glazed wall onto a large covered balcony looking down towards the end of the garden.

The contrast within is between a very utilitarian style and architectural forms deriving from great Western architecture and this sense of austerity and grandeur carries on outside. There is no garden as such, rather the floor of the main level of the house continues through the picture window and along a promenade to a small concrete pergola and basin that presents a surprise

Casa Kalman, Ticino, Switzerland. Despite an emerging Classicism in Ticinese architecture and an almost equal interest in local vernaculars, not to mention the influence of Kahn, the Casa Kalmann is firmly in the spirit of the Swiss Le Corbusier. In a variation on the Pavilion de l'Esprit Nouveau, Snozzi has designed a double-height space where the mezzanine is turned through 90 degrees, thus allowing the principal bedroom a balcony created by insetting a glazed wall in a design that shares a concern with shelter with Botta's Casa Bianchi.

Casa Kalman, Ticino, Switzerland. Snozzi's use of concrete, metal-framed glazing, simple rails and plainly laid tiles also recalls Le Corbusier; the terrace with its pavilion could owe something to the roof terraces of Le Corbusier's early villas, but it is as indebted to classical garden design of the 17th and early 18th centuries for the device of a walk where the view is obscured until the correct moment, as in the Villa Gamberaia at Florence or the Rievaulx Terrace in Yorkshire *(below)*. Snozzi was fascinated by how local builders placed buildings in the most advantageous position relative to climate and geography, and had made a special study of these features. This work must have had some effect on his designs for the Casa Kalman since, despite the exposed position of the pavilion, it is, like many farm buildings, unusually 'out of the weather'.

view of the whole of Locarno and the surrounding Lake Maggiore. It is in the relationship between the house and its pavilion that another level of architectural complexity is introduced. The wall facing the lowest part of the site runs straight at around 45 degrees to the high, virtually blank, outer wall of the house whereas the wall on the inner-slope side of the site follows a radius that continues from the pavilion right along the wall of the house. This simple contrast of angles and curves creates a distinct formality in the sense of the relationship of the house and its pavilion that recalls the formal gardens of Tuscan palazzi and, *inter alia*, has the effect of partially and temptingly obscuring the view of the pavilion from the house. Equally the virtually blank side walls of the house that face the road create a very private space within what is necessarily a very public site.

The most striking feeling that is created by the structure is a sense of simultaneous largeness and smallness, modesty and grandeur. The utilitarian is combined with a wealth of cultural references to the Renaissance villa or the 18th-century gardens of England – in particular, the magnificent, and yet pointless, terrace at Rievaulx, Yorkshire, where separate dining and withdrawing temples are joined by a promenade giving views of a ruined Cistercian abbey in the valley below.

Snozzi, like Campi, has taken the language of Modernism and, without diluting its purpose, added the classical devices developed in the Renaissance to give architecture a rhetoric that transcends the manner of its articulation. This use of the classical lexicon of devices available to the architect is in marked contrast to the naked and unimaginative historicism using similar devices that emerged in Britain and America in the late 1970s and onward into the 1990s.

Above: Casa Kalman, Ticino, Switzerland.
Snozzi was interested in the use of path and
entries, and the vistas that they create. This
aesthetic is expressed frequently in the Casa
Kalman where it is almost possible to see from the
end of the garden to the back of the house.
Contrary to expectations, the effect of this is to
create a sense of space rather than emphasise
the restricted scale of the house.

Right: Casa Kalman, Ticino, Switzerland.
Though there is a spartan quality to the interiors of the house, in part this was specified by the owners. Snozzi's design concerns itself with the provision of viewpoints perhaps more than with the beauty of where those views are seen from. The small size of the house makes it important that the architecture provides as many interesting outlooks as possible,. The view from the kitchen is across ground lightly planted with small trees.

Left: Casa Kalman, Ticino, Switzerland. Rather than using stairs like a spiral, that are compact in their footprint, Snozzi uses long stairs to create either expectation, as in the case of the entrance to the house where a long unlit stair leads up to the light of the main living space, or as here to create a complex vista using two long windows. Similarly, the bridge across the stairwell, another Snozzi motif, creates a point from which the exterior pavilion can be contemplated.

Casa Kalman, Ticino, Switzerland. The severity of the interior spaces, the use of plain, hard surfaces, the exaggerated exposure of elements like radiators and the use of simple, industrial-looking features, like the metal glazing bars and the welded wire balustrade on the first floor above the living room, are all elements that have their origins in Le Corbusier's villas of the 1920s.

Hopkins House

Michael and Patty Hopkins

Hampstead, London, UK   1975-76

Hampstead sits above the smog and summer humidity of central London and this has made it a refuge from the city for the past two centuries. Separating Hampstead from Highgate is the wide slope of Hampstead Heath where the Fleet River rises, fed by springs and ponds that have long been used for bathing. At the weekend the heath is the scene of a constant *paseo* resembling a cross between Central Park and the Bois de Boulogne. Between the well-heeled pleasures of Hampstead's shops and restaurants and the rural urbanity of the heath alternate quiet tree-lined streets of faintly artistic Victorian solidity and earlier thoroughfares of white stuccoed terraces behind catalpas, large magnolias and wisteria. Peppered amongst these archetypes of London's salubrity are some of the city's Modernist houses, like Ernö Goldfinger's building on Willow Road (1939). These are monuments to Hampstead's artistic intellectual population, which gave refuge to Gropius and Breuer, among others, en route to America. Near both Goldfinger's and the poet Keats' house is the Hopkins House invisibly slotted in between brick and stucco terraces.

The house lies behind dense, dark trees on a steeply falling site that makes the two-storey structure seem like a bungalow from the street, but from the rear of the first storey the mature garden, which includes a giant ash, a large mock orange and a medlar shading the patio, seems far below. Perhaps typically of London houses, the Hopkins House was designed to be cheap. As Michael Hopkins said, he wanted to find out, 'How much we can get for how little'. So despite, or perhaps because of, the good fortune of buying a double-width site with previous planning permission in a fantastic position in one of London's most desirable streets the Hopkins House was built for £20,000. This was achieved through the use of components and technology more usually employed in constructing out-of-town industrial estates.

The design of the house is extremely simple being essentially two glass-faced boxes that together measure approximately 12 x 10 x 6 metres. The structure is supported by a very light steel frame based on a 4 x 2-metre module of 63 x 63-millimetre columns and 250-millimetre-deep lattice beams to support the roof and first floor. This is cross-braced at the second and sixth modules of the street and garden facades, and strengthening is also used on the ground floor below the point where an entrance bridge joins the structure of the house. Thus, within the house the only necessary interruptions to the space are the spiral staircase in the centre of the house and eight thin steel columns that divide the house into three 4-metre-wide bays. The bays are further divided by Venetian blinds that lie between the columns and run from

Below: **Hopkins House, London, UK.** Though the separation of interior and exterior seems minimal from within, from the exterior the reflective glass and the dark interior accentuate the light frame and with it the sense of overall form and proportion of the house. These conform to the conventions of the traditional classicised English villa of the 18th century, with its overall squat rectangular form and carefully proportioned modules that fall into six bays.

Above and top: Hopkins House, London, UK.
By using a very light structure wherever possible, including single-glazed windows, the Hopkins created the most minimal of envelopes to separate themselves from the outside environment, and as 50 per cent of the glazed facade can be fully opened the separation of interior and exterior can be almost removed. On the upper floor this sense of openness is emphasised by the combination of height and the almost invisible restraint from falling provided by the stainless-steel wire stretched across the opening like the safety rails on a yacht.

the front to the back of the house and effectively separate the bays when they are dropped. The street and garden facades are made from 24 glass panels of which 12 slide open to their full width. One of these forms the front door to the house on the first floor, which is accessed via the light steel bridge from the street. The side walls and roof of the building are made from corrugated-steel sheets sandwiched around fibreglass insulation and heat is provided by a hot-air system that passes along exposed piping at ceiling level. Lighting is provided by a tracklight system fitted to the lattice joists and electricity is supplied via floor sockets. The service areas of the house – the bathrooms, kitchen and utilities – are all housed in three modules made from melamine-laminated panels that sit on the floor of the main structure. At the centre of

the eastern bay of the house are two bathrooms, over and below each other, while on the west bay of the ground floor is the kitchen–utility module. The kitchen faces the garden while the side of the module facing the external side wall is given over to utilities and storage. At the heart of this module is the heating equipment for the house. In front of the south-facing kitchen side of the module is a waist-height 3 x 1 x 1-metre storage unit.

The effect of these modules is to divide up the open space of the house so that, though open, the use of the house is divided into six sections in three bays. The western bay on the upper floor forms an office area for the owners. The central area on the upper level gives access to the front door, the stairs and a sitting area overlooking the garden. The eastern bay on the upper floor is a suite of spaces divided off from the rest of the upper floor by blinds and from each other by the central bathroom module which, with the blinds down, creates a corridor between the master bedroom overlooking the garden and a dressing room facing the street. Downstairs the space is divided so that the eastern and western bays on the street side are bedrooms with fixed melamine-laminate walls. In the centre bay the walls of the bedrooms are used to support shelves for children's books and toys making the area in between effectively a playroom that is divided from the rest of the floor by a Venetian blind. The eastern bay of the ground floor at the garden end is a TV room. Next to this is the entrance to the garden and then the centre bay, and the western bay on the garden side becomes the kitchen–dining area. Thus, though the house has the potential of being fully open and, through the use of screens and blinds, is very flexible in the definition of space, it in fact conforms to a conventional plan of a medium-sized family house with open-planned living areas.

Remarkably, the house retains its original colour scheme of silver blinds, grey–silver exterior walls, grey carpets throughout, and matched fitted grey Pirelli flooring in the kitchen and matched fitted grey foot-brushing carpet by the doors. The melamine-laminated wall panels and utility modules are in white while the metal frame, stairs and exterior ironmongery is in mid-blue. The internal ironmongery is either in white or brushed steel. There is also a considerable amount of the original furniture, which appears only to have been altered by replacements of some old Eames chairs for newer ones and the addition of some Magistretti sofas designed in the 1970s.

Though the house owes something to American precedents like Mies' Farnsworth House (1946–50) and the Eames House (1945–9), at the time it was felt to be, like Piano and Rogers' Centre Pompidou (1971–7), a new

Hopkins House, London, UK. The structural elements of the house are painted bright blue, as are the stairs, which serves to make a point of their lightness. This motif is maintained by the frequent use of metal Venetian blinds to divide up the interior space and the use of corrugated materials which by their profile signify thinness. At the same time, through their visual similarity to the corrugated form of the roof, the blinds borrow some of its signified solidity, thus helping the viewer accept their role as a wall rather than a window shade.

departure in British-designed architecture. It has since been variously labelled Ad Hoc, High Tech and Late Modern depending on the moment of analysis. The terms each have their own validity. The first two refer to the aesthetic use of industrially produced fittings and the modularisation of areas like the bathrooms. The last term implies that, among a few other buildings of the mid and late 1970s, the Hopkins House had found a new synthesis for Modernist architecture. However, the combination of the recessive economic situation, which in part generated the building, and the cultural retreat into nostalgia that marked the end of the 1970s and the 1980s effectively made the Hopkins House a much cited precursor of the later, and more conservative, Modernist Revival in domestic architecture despite the success of this type of building in commercial architecture.

The most significant factor in the Hopkins House is its flexibility both within the existing structure and in the design of the exterior envelope that allows extra space to be added to the building, either to the facade or the top. But it is this flexibility of the structure and the mode of living possible inside the building that indicate its age. Flexibility was gained at the expense of what would now be seen as a luxury concomitant with the location of the house. In its original form the design combined an egalitarian social fluidity in the plan of its spaces with a very utilitarian approach to all the service functions of the house, particularly the bathrooms and utility area and the lack of storage and parking space. It is interesting that while the Hopkins House is more architecturally modern it is the contemporary, and more conservative, American and Swiss houses with their more elaborate and segregated plans that are more socially modern.

Above: Hopkins House, London, UK. The primary colours are set against a neutral palette of greys and silver that defines the envelope of the internal spaces, and their combination gives an almost early Renaissance effect of carefully drawn three-dimensional objects in a landscape. While many 1970s designs made use of primary colours their use here as highlights in an essentially neutral environment is a precursor of the designs of the 1980s.

Left: Hopkins House, London, UK. Throughout the house the owners have maintained the theme of lightness with a careful selection of Modern furniture designs from the 1930s through to the 1970s, all of which appear to float above the floor. This, with the blinds and the continuous carpet, gives the impression of a wall-to-wall openness that makes the house seem huge. With some exceptions, the furnishings have a strong sculptural quality that is often combined with a primary colour or black or white.

DIFFUSION

This section takes as its organising principle the idea that the architectural style of any given period, in this case the 1970s, is a necessarily complex map of aesthetic innovation, emulation and conservatism. At any point throughout the decade it would be possible to find some very innovative architecture, rather more architecture that emulated the successful innovations of earlier architecture and much more architecture that conservatively applied the most tried and trusted architectural solutions, some of which may go back decades. This process can be characterised as one of diffusion in the sense of a spread of elements of (architectural) culture to another region or people.

Diffusion

The concept of diffusion as applied to the aesthetics of domestic architecture is particularly useful in considering the architecture of the 1970s because the decade followed on from a sustained period of widespread architectural innovation that followed the Second World War. The result of this was that in the decade before the Post-Modernism of the 1980s the Modernism of the post-war years had grown from a type of architecture only found in certain, very localised and socially specific, parts of Europe and America to a truly intercontinental style. A case in point is Greece, the site of two of the examples listed in this section, where, despite its proximity to Italy which had a tradition of Modernist architecture dating back to the late 1920s, because of slow economic and political development the architects and the market for aesthetically Modern architecture only emerged in the late 1960s and blossomed in the 1970s.

Equally, by the 1970s, within the vast geographic hegemony of Modernism there were even degrees of diffusion, which were dependent on a highly architecturally innovative local context, apparent in the most up-to-date architecture. For example, in New York State, the site of De Vido's Sametz House, the innovative forms of Modernist architecture characterised by the work that the New York Five developed in the 1960s became widely diffused through the 1970s by architects working for the well-educated professional clients that formed the state's market for progressive architecture.

Though the examples of the diffusion of new architectural aesthetics in New York State and Greece are almost polar opposites of the model, a more familiar case is found in the example of the Haus Neumann in Berlin, where diffusion of architectural aesthetics is conditioned by more familiar commercial speculative considerations. Berlin may be taken to represent a mature Modernist architectural environment where innovative design has a long history matched by the conservative tendencies of the general population. What is unusual about Berlin is that, notwithstanding the city's long association with Modernist architecture, the effects of the Second World War and then partition had the effect of delaying the post-war consumerist boom until the 1970s. This delay resulted in an architectural milieu that combined development of the most up-to-date architecture with less innovative styles in the same locales, each reflecting different sectors of the market. While a small number of architects were able to find clients who wanted the most contemporary architecture there was a much larger market for an architecture of moderate and familiar Modernism, which synthesised elements from previous decades in an attractive and reassuringly familiar interpretation of Modern design. The significance of this more middle-of-the-road architecture and of the diffusion of architectural style generally is that they do not show the most extreme aspects of 1970s domestic architecture but a more complex and widespread picture of the decade. What gives the architecture of the 1970s some of its distinct flavour and interest is that there was a new spread of stylistic elements available to a wider public in more countries than the diffused architectural tropes available in the 1960s. The less-innovative architecture of the 1970s displayed a different lack of innovation to that of the 1960s. It was less homogeneous because of the increase in aesthetic experimentation at the more theoretical end of architecture in the 1960s and early 1970s, and there was more of it in more places because of the increasing development of the world's economy.

At Scharfe Lanke in Spandau on the edge of Berlin are two buildings built by the same developer. Haus Plettner was the eponymous developer's home and next door was a commercial development of four terraced houses, of which Haus Neumann is the example featured here. Both lead down to an arm of the River Havel but that is where the similarity ends. The row of which Haus Neumann is a part is a familiar modern Berliner ensemble of white-painted concrete facades articulated by projecting covered entrance stairs

Haus Plettner, Berlin, Germany. This house with its extreme Brutalist formality shows, by comparison with its neighbours, the difference between the 1970s speculative market and one-off architectural taste.

and lobbies. It refers back to the German Modernism of the 1920s and the expensive survivors of this period in the wooded suburbs between Spandau and Berlin. Haus Plettner on the other hand is in the international Brutalist style more common in the public architecture of Berlin, such as the Kongresshalle by Ralf Schuler and Ursulina Schuler-Witte (1973–9).

The differences in architectural language of the Haus Plettner and the Haus Neumann do not represent a temporal difference in style since they were erected one after the other between 1970 and 1974, with the Haus Plettner being built first. They differ because one is a speculative project and the other a personal statement. Haus Neumann is part of a block designed to please a broad spectrum of taste that aspired to own 'architecture' whereas the developer's own house next door represents the owner's desire to separate himself from his clients through the self-conscious selection of a more minority taste in domestic architecture. The same differences can be found in the houses built for the developer Leslie Bilsby by Patrick Gwynne and the houses designed for his SPAN company by Eric Lyons. Like SPAN houses, in many ways the Haus Neumann is more liveable than its developer's own home. It is less intrusive, less dominant and is designed to flatter the sense of wellbeing of the inhabitants. It combines contemporary detailing with a locally familiar Modernist typology and, as was increasingly true of 1970s architecture, care was taken to offer what in automotive design was then called 'creature comforts' like the freestanding, circular open fire in the living room, which stood as a signifier for the more leisured life of the

Gorman House, Long Island, New York. This tiny beach house shows the minimal elements of the New York / Long Island weekender vernacular that developed in the mid-1960s.

1970s future. Moreover, if considered as a product rather than architecture, it is evident that Haus Neumann follows Raymond Loewy's observation that design should not run too far ahead of established public taste. The freestanding fire is emblematic of this principle since, although it seems very exotic in Haus Neumann, it is a rhetorical gesture towards the more radical, more open Modernism that formed the setting for earlier examples from the late 1950s. This is not to say that Haus Neumann is not really uniquely of the 1970s, since such a commercial project was unlikely to have been built in Berlin in the 1960s, but rather that it represents what was possible and desirable in the 1970s in its particular context.

This diffusion of architectural trends is as present in the high-standard architecture of the period as in the basic developers' housing, particularly in contexts where there was either a strong local architectural environment or where, by contrast, there was little architectural culture. Cases in point are the architecture of New York's rich weekend diaspora and its Athenian counterpart.

Greek Modern architecture was in its infancy in the 1970s because, in comparison to other European countries, Greece's 20th-century development was held back by a prolonged period of war from 1939 to 1949. Thus, it was only in the late 1950s and 1960s that Greek architectural education began to embrace Modernism, and only in the mid- to late 1960s that the first generations of post-war architects, and clients for that matter, began to emerge in any numbers. The architects of the late 1960s generation of graduates were trained by people involved in the Congrès International d'Architecture Moderne (CIAM) and moved in a progressive intellectual climate that looked beyond conservative Greek traditionalism towards Europe, America and Japan for its inspiration. Because of this much Greek Modernism emulates the trends of distant Modernisms in a highly gestural and culturally symbolic manner.

The work of Athenian architect Alexandros Tombazis is representative of the way in which Greek architects assimilated and rapidly diffused a succession of international architectural aesthetics during the rapid modernisation of Athens that has taken place since the 1960s, continuing a process that began in the 1950s.

In the 1960s American architectural styles dominated the homes built for wealthy Athenians seeking retreats from the dense urbanity of an exponentially enlarged Athens, and Angelino-style bungalows still line the out-of-town roads by the sea and the older suburbs of the city. Tombazis' first house, which was built while he was still a student, followed this trend for a rather conventional American Modernism, but a few years later when the owner of this first house commissioned a beach house from him he adopted a much more contemporary style and the new Svolos House was an extreme assembly of Brutalist modules. By the late 1970s Tombazis had built up a well-established practice and was beginning to specialise in the infant technology of ecological climate control. In 1979 he designed a house in the new suburb of Ekali where the interior climate was controlled by the design of the form of the house and its relation to its site. This was the first design of this kind in Greece and also featured a novel, at that time, atrium. The design

Svolos House, Kifissia, Greece. This house was designed while its architect was still a student and shows both the quality of his design and, when compared with his subsequent *oeuvre*, his predilection for working in ever-changing contemporary idioms.

of the rest of the building employed an Adhocist, almost utilitarian, aesthetic, which featured in many northern European public buildings of the period.

Tombazis' practice may seem stylistically derivative despite being technically innovative, but this would be to ignore important determinants on that practice. At a personal level Tombazis is unconcerned about style, while at the same time committed to novelty, and has said, 'I have no patience with personal egoism such as who thought of an idea first,' and, 'One of my deep satisfactions while practising architecture is that it never ceases to evolve. It is always one continuous and broadening process.'[1] At another level Tombazis' practice and his attitude reflect a pragmatic adaptation to rapid developments that take place in more dynamic architectural economies. It demonstrates an acceptance of the reality that, in order to maintain the dynamism of his or her practice, an architect on the edges of architectural culture will act as an agent for the diffusion of new architectural designs, and that the quality of this practice will depend on the skill with which genuine advances in architecture are recognised over superficial aesthetic fashions.

By contrast, few places could be so central to the development of architecture in the past 50 years as New York State. The huge wealth of New York and the general cultural ascendancy of the United States has created not only the great architecture of Manhattan but also a huge body of innovative domestic architecture. Long Island, in particular, has been the focus of architectural innovation in domestic design from the late 19th century onwards. While the early development of New Yorkers' houses on Long Island was of large mansions, as have been the more recent developments of the 1980s and 1990s, there was a period when lack of development on the island and a relative affluence among young professional New Yorkers fostered a boom in small architect-designed weekend houses. This began in the 1950s

House on National Road, Ayii Theodori, Greece. This house from the mid-1960s is typical of the influence of American house design on modern Greek architecture prior to the 1970s.

when Long Island developed a reputation as a Bohemian refuge for artists like Jackson Pollock. This in turn led to an influx throughout the 1960s of young, affluent city escapees seeking a simple life, at the weekend at least. The island also attracted young architects who could develop their practices through small domestic projects for broad-minded young clients. Architects who are now internationally famous, like Eisenman, Meier and Graves, developed their practices in New York in the 1960s, and helped generate the New York architectural aesthetic of extreme cubic formalism described by Eisenman as 'cardboard architecture'[2] and Tafuri as 'sublime uselessness',[3] and 'form without utopia'.[4] The aesthetic dominated the new Long Island weekend architecture that was the target of Tafuri's remarks, while Eisenman's comment refers to the appearance of the buildings which were often cubic, made from apparently thin materials and punctuated by large cut-out openings. The style had its roots not only in the abstraction of the architects' drawings, but also in the balloon-framed, cedar-sided and shingled vernacular of the East Coast. This style was apparent as early as 1964 at Amagansett, when Charles Gwathmey built his parents a house in an essentially cubic form with neat, formal, geometric additions and cutaways.

By 1972, when the Long Island Expressway reached Riverhead at the edge of the formerly reasonably remote Hamptons, a building boom ensued and the style practised by locally well-known architects like the Neskis and Al De Vido effectively developed into a local vernacular. An essential part of the style was the provision of constantly varying views, and this accounts for certain repetitive elements of the genre: the tendency to build high to gain a view, and an ascending procession of interior levels around the structure accessing piercings in the skin that afforded long vistas rather than corresponding to 'normal' expectations of where windows ought to be. The popularity of the style lay in its economy, the combination of local materials and craft for construction and an abstraction of form that declared its intellectuality, its roots in International Modernism, for all to see. What is most interesting about the 1970s architecture of Long Island is the sheer number of houses built, which in itself created a large local architectural profession working in a genuinely Modernist and modern vernacular diffused from a few well-known early 1960s designs. By the late 1970s the style still had a currency, and had become diffused throughout New York's weekender hinterland as far as Connecticut. In 1979 Al De Vido was using it to build in the neglected purlieus of the Hudson valley and then, with the advent of Post-Modernism, it all came to a halt – but only as a Modernist domestic vernacular of the New York weekend diaspora. In international architecture the style retained a presence in the intellectualism of Deconstructionist architecture.

1   Taken from an autobiographical note in Alexandros Tombazis, *Meletitiki,*
     Alexandros N Tombazis and Associates Architects Ltd (Athens), 1997.

2   Quoted in Alastair Gordon, *Weekend Utopia: Modern Living in the Hamptons*,
     Princeton Architectural Press (New York), 2001, p 128.

3   *Ibid.*

4   *Ibid.*

Haus Neumann

Dieter Frowein and Jurgen Sawade
Scharfe Lanke, Spandau, Berlin, Germany   1972-74

Scharfe Lanke is one of the inlets of the River Havel as it passes through the low, wooded hinterland of Berlin. Since the early years of the last century, the city's riverine landscape has become the focus of genteel suburban development based around the leisure pursuits of gardening, walking and water sports. Until the end of the 1960s Scharfe Lanke was mainly surrounded by small summer houses and their allotment gardens, and also played host to three sailing clubs. During the 1970s, as Berlin expanded after years of post-war recovery, such outer areas became the focus of middle-class housing development as they had a rural aspect yet were within 20 minutes of the city centre. Scharfe Lanke and the neighbouring Pichelsburg were some of the last areas to be redeveloped and this may in part be because they lay very close to the Berlin Wall.

The land in Scharfe Lanke that forms the plot for Haus Neumann, and its neighbour Haus Plettner, was purchased by a property developer and the site divided. Haus Plettner was built by Jan and Rolf Rave between 1971 and 1972 as a house for the developer, while next door a row of four speculative houses, designed by Dieter Frowein and Jurgen Sawade, were built on a larger plot. These were built as in a block, or terrace, running down to the lake. The access road to the houses separated them from Haus Plettner and also gave access to a slipway and moorings that were part of the development. On the other side and between the end of the row and the waterfront lie communal gardens, including a waterside swimming pool. Each property has access to the gardens by means of a wide flight of steps leading down from the main floor of the house.

The four small houses are identical in plan and follow the sort of town-house plan that was common in Britain in the 1970s with an exterior style that reflects Germany's Modernist heritage. The ground floor is occupied by a garage towards the road side with a 'workroom' to the rear that, in this case, has been turned into a living–study room by the addition of large windows facing the garden and a spiral staircase giving access from the floor above.

The reason for this is that the principal floor of each house is the first floor, which is reached by a covered and individual stairway from the road outside, the lower floor being originally accessed by means of the garage door only. The main floor has a lobby, cloakroom and stairs to the second floor towards the front. Behind these a double-width door leads to a fitted kitchen overlooking the garden and a living room with floor-to-ceiling doors that open onto a veranda that runs the width of the property, which in turn leads to a very wide, metal-framed wooden stairway leading down to the gardens. In the

Above: **Haus Neumann, Berlin, Germany.**
The very stark colour and geometry of the front facade of the Scharfe Lanke houses is in a well-established German vernacular dating back to the 1920s when the essentialist geometry of German Modernism first emerged.

Opposite: **Haus Neumann, Berlin, Germany.**
The rear elevation is in complete semiotic contrast to the entrance facade. Here, mute geometry is replaced by an almost Art Deco celebration of the nautical.

centre of the living room is a freestanding circular open fire, fire hood and wide chimney, which is the focal point of the room. Upstairs a wide landing open at one side up to skylights and down to the main floor, gives access to a top-lit bathroom and two bedrooms overlooking the gardens. At the waterside end the last house in the row has a large vacuum-moulded window in the living-room wall giving the owners a view of the lake.

The kitchens of the houses are fitted in a line along the wall and have an inset electric hob and separate built-in oven. The backsplashes are tiled in 4-centimetre-square tiles in an orange-brown typical of the period. The bathroom has the same colour tiling, and fashionable fittings of the period like the non-pedestal, double washbasin. Throughout the house flush panel doors are used and the handles are of the simple nylon design, often in primary colours, black and white, that was almost a universal feature of architect-designed houses of the 1970s. The walls of the interior are white.

Stylistically the houses at Scharfe Lanke are interesting because they combine small scale and a number of disparate architectural elements that signify larger, more luxurious architecture. They are modest in the basic form but have a number of significant features that carry the otherwise plain design. The public exterior appears as a series of blank volumes facing the public road and gives an impression of a very severe Modernism. The private garden side and the lake frontage are different again and strive for a nautical feel through the use of white stucco, the round 'bubble window', in itself a very 'fashionable' element of the design, and long runs of windows above steel-balustered open stairways that combined give the impression of a small, docked liner when seen from the lake.

These features and the swimming pool and moorings straightforwardly signify a lifestyle beyond the fact of the house's position by a lake. Such signifiers are not limited to the exterior. The most striking feature of the interiors is the simplicity of the rooms and their fittings, with the very large exception of the freestanding fireplace in the centre of the living room. These spectacular fires were popular features of 1960s and 1970s homes in Europe and America but usually in much larger surroundings. Their inclusion in the Scharfe Lanke houses shows the architects' desire to give them a symbolic quality by including the owners in the world of contemporary and leisured affluence that the aura of these fireplaces engenders.

Disappointingly, three of the four houses have removed the central fireplace, but fortunately in our example the owners commissioned a specially designed sofa that matches and emphasises the role of this freestanding fire.

Opposite: **Haus Neumann, Berlin, Germany.**
Inside the architects move from nautical symbols to one of the most desirable of post-war Modernist icons, the freestanding fireplace.

Left: **Haus Neumann, Berlin, Germany.** In keeping with the implications of many of the features of their house, the owners opened up the kitchen to create a continuous living space and set a similarly appropriate nautical spiral stair in the floor, giving access to a room developed out of a garage work area.

In addition they have enhanced the sense of space on the main floor by removing a large section of the kitchen wall, which has created a continuous space right across the veranda side of the house into which they have inserted the spiral staircase to the new study. One, perhaps unforeseen, benefit of this addition is that the volume of light is increased in both the study and the living area. These conversions to the original plan have had the effect of realising the potential of the lower parts of the house.

The houses at Scharfe Lanke represent a time when the futuristic and leisured homes and lifestyles available to the very rich became accessible to much less wealthy home buyers – a point where there was some democratisation of the good life of yachts and swimming pools framed in a modern idiom.

Opposite: **Haus Neumann, Berlin, Germany.** The bathroom is typical of the international approach to these rooms in the 1970s. Bathrooms, though less basic than those of the 1960s, were still rather small and relegated to isolated interior spaces that were top-lit. The frequent use of strong colours for bathrooms in the 1970s, often yellows, browns and oranges, was to get away from the clinical look of the 1960s designs. The use of built-in units, based on kitchen models, became increasingly common in the 1970s and presaged the emergence of the kitchen and bathroom as major areas of expenditure in house designs that emerged in the 1980s.

Svolos House

Alexandros Tombazis

Ayii Theodori, Gerania, Greece   1975

Alexandros Tombazis is a remarkably flexible architect who has worked in many idioms, and nowhere is this better seen than in the comparison between the Svolos main residence in the wealthy Athens suburb of Pangrati and the Svolos holiday home at Ayii Theodori on the old National Road to Corinth. The first residence, constructed in the late 1960s, is very clearly based on American prototypes with its wide, land-hugging profile, open planning and combination of luxurious and rustic materials. The house at Ayii Theodori, by the sea, could be by a different architect and displays a spectacular late modern combination of Brutalist materials and sculptural form. It shows a cultural optimism in the future that elsewhere in Europe was on the wane in 1975, and reflects the emergence of a new wealthy and culturally engaged middle class in a nation previously dominated by the culturally conservative elite. The owner who commissioned Tombazis to design two houses was both an athlete, carrying the torch for Greece at the 1948 London Olympics, and the owner of a stainless steel fabrication company and represented the kind of Reconstructionist spirit that by the 1970s was fast disappearing elsewhere in Europe.

The house at Ayii Theodori lies between the old National Road and the sea of the gulf of Salamis between Athens and Corinth. The house, in common with many Greek summer houses, is occupied mainly at Easter and throughout August and is set in a traditional agricultural garden of vegetable plots and fruit trees, including olives, oranges and lemons. The house stands in their midst like the palace of some *Star Wars* despot, its main door being approached by a long, concrete ramp planted in places with grass. The plan of the house is remarkably simple. The main part stands on stilts above two separate guest wings, each with sleeping and washing facilities. Between them lies an open courtyard looking down across a lawn to the sea 75 metres beyond. Above, the main body of the house is divided into three sections – a central loggia is flanked by a living room and kitchen on one side and a master bedroom and bathroom on the other.

The grandiloquence and sculptural exuberance of the wide facade belies the simplicity of the plan and the fact that the structure is really only one room deep. The exaggerated exterior articulation of the Brutalist structure disappears inside in favour of large and simply defined spaces, with the exception of the living room where a specially commissioned ceramic mural runs the full width of a large, open fireplace and dominates the room. Elsewhere the house is very simple and reflects the modern Greek vernacular use of crudely finished, white-painted concrete and greeny-blue polished

Svolos House, Ayii Theodori, Greece.
Compared to its neighbours the Svolos House represents a radical departure from the ranch-house bungalow style that dominated Greek Modernism in the 1960s. With parallels in the architecture of Expo 67 in Montreal, British Brutalism and Japanese Metabolism, the Svolos House is an ambitious statement of confidence in Modernism built at a time when the movement was collapsing in Britain and America.

DIFFUSION

Above: **Svolos House, Ayii Theodori, Greece.** This highly gestural module houses the service rooms at the Svolos House. The steel 'vent' is in fact a window and is particularly appropriate as a symbol of the interior space.

Opposite: **Svolos House, Ayii Theodori, Greece.** Much of the living at the Svolos summer house takes place outside, to the extent that the kitchen has its own access to the garden. Because of this lack of distinction between interior and exterior living the house is as much looked at by its owners as looked from, and this in part accounts for the Baroque lavishness of its form – it is as much, if not more, sculpture than dwelling.

Karystos stone floors. Doors are made from the equally well-established modern vernacular material iroko, as are the shutters to the radiused and modular form window apertures. In the kitchen there is the unique feature of a spiral staircase, set in an opening steel casement, leading down to the garden, in recognition of the need for easy access between the kitchen and garden in summer when much of the household living takes place outside.

The furniture of the house is still original and was commissioned by the owner's wife from an Athens furniture designer and made to high standards in emulation of Scandinavian originals, though the colour scheme of semi-matt lime greens, orangey reds and off-whites owes more to Mediterranean fashions than to those of Scandinavia. Elsewhere in the house the colour scheme is dominated by traditional Greek whites and deep blues contrasted with natural woods, but in the kitchen and dining areas the dominant colour is yellow-green, which works well in the harsh light of the Greek coast.

A noticeable feature of the Ayii Theodori beach house is its genuine Brutalism. Built with the intention of maximising style and scale within a limited budget, it embraces a very pragmatic coarseness of material and finish, which is very much in the spirit of Le Corbusier's *béton brut* of the 1950s. In many respects the fitting out of the house, particularly the electrics, seems crude, but it should be remembered that the architect was given free rein within the specified budget and thus any rawness in the construction and finish are there because the form of the architecture has been given absolute priority.

As with many other houses that we visited, it is in immaculate condition and in this case the exterior in particular seems as new, and has in fact been improved by the growing of plants on and around the building, in particular the grass on the access ramp. The overall effect of the house at maturity is that of a Brutalist sculpture, which stands out from the various versions of American-inspired bungalow homes that surround it. Overall the architecture has a sense of freedom and exuberant experimentation not found elsewhere in Europe, and although this is in part due to the character of the owners it may also be because for the Greeks the 1970s were a time of new freedom and expansion after a very long period of recovery. This was a time when Greek architecture was running through the gamut of post-war styles and exaggerating them to dramatic and showy effect in celebration of joining the modern world. While many in Europe had begun to doubt the benefits of Modernism, Greece was just beginning to revel in its ideas.

Opposite: Svolos House, Ayii Theodori, Greece.
The two interior spaces that are given more than the basic attention that characterises the rest of the Svolos House are the living area and the kitchen. The former has the characteristic Tombazis-type fireplace, and is furnished in a modern interpretation of traditional Greek spaces where guests are received and indoor family life takes place. Modern though this space and its furnishings appear, its style is Mediterranean in origin and was adopted by Modernism in recognition of its leisured informality.

Above: Svolos House, Ayii Theodori, Greece.
While there were established modern styles for kitchens and living rooms, bedroom furniture, perhaps particularly in Greece, was dominated by the old-fashioned notion of the suite. Though it now looks rather odd, the custom-built bedroom furniture at the Svolos House is an attempt to modernise the bedroom. It is interesting because in its form it emulates the moulded plastic furniture then produced in Italy – though in this case in solid lacquered wood – and the modularised Brutalism of the house.

Right: Svolos House, Ayii Theodori, Greece.
The kitchen is the factory for the constant eating that goes with vacation living, as well as providing another focus for the social transactions of the house. Svolos made his money from the manufacture of metal forms for the German kitchen-fitters Franke, and his kitchen has a large scale unusual in many Greek homes. The furniture and units were all custom-built because, at that time, this was easier than providing a factory-made kitchen. The bright colour of the furniture also represents a commitment to an international Modernism since it eschews the almost universal Greek national taste for bright turquoise blue.

Sofianos House

Alexandros Tombazis

Ekali, Kifissia, Athens, Greece   1979

Ekali, near the wealthy Athens suburb Kifissia, rises steeply above the plain to the north-east of Athens conveniently near the new E Venizelos airport. With its well-manicured roads, high fences and discreet guards some parts of Ekali have a distinctly Angelino feel, and this is enhanced by streets of oleander hedges and rambling villas looking out towards bare mountains over a plain that is becoming increasingly de-agriculturalised.

In the late 1970s the area was largely undeveloped, with few metalled roads and no new airport, so the decision of the owner Sofianos, a forestry and timber merchant, to build his house here was prescient. Despite his father's view that such a project was a vain waste of time, he engaged Tombazis as his architect because of the latter's reputation for integrity.

An immediate problem with the site, which is on a steep rock hillside, was its preparation for construction, which required blasting rather than excavation. This should not give the false impression that the site was reduced to a *tabula rasa* since the rear of the villa is built hard up against the natural fall of the hill and its dense vegetation, which is part of the design.

The Sofianos House was the first modern house in Greece to use passive solar heating; that is, it was designed to be heated by the sun but without the use of solar panels as used in Tombazis' own home, Helios 1, in Trapeza. The need for solar heat meant that the design of the villa fell into two sections, both of which were clearly expressed in the structure. The main rooms are on two storeys facing the valley, with the upper range overhanging the lower one to create a veranda on the ground floor. The upper rooms give onto a deep landing or mezzanine that runs the full length of the house. Enveloping the rear of the villa over the mezzanine and the hall below is a large, fully glazed sloping roof, and the resulting atrium provides the ambient heating for the house. The boscage on the steep hill immediately behind the villa, which includes a full-sized plane tree growing over the roof of the atrium, serves to moderate the extremes of heat and cold that would result if the area were barren.

The effect of the atrium and its proximity to dense greenery is to create a sense from within the building that one is surrounded by a forest, which is in direct contrast to the hot and dry landscapes visible from the front veranda of the house. The psychological coolness of the atrium area forms the first impression of the villa as the visitor enters the house from the harsh light of the street entrance. Stairs rise from the ground to the first floor through the atrium, and passage from room to room, with the exception of transit from the living to dining areas, is via this large, green space.

Sofianos House, Athens, Greece. The Sofianos House combines luxury with asceticism in the contrasting combination of its restrained board-marked concrete structure punctuated by off-the-peg manufactured windows, doors and architectural ironmongery, and its swimming pool which features its own lift and a 'cascade'. Both its features and style represent Modernism on the edge of the Post-Modern where restraint and expressiveness seem in irreconcilable tension.

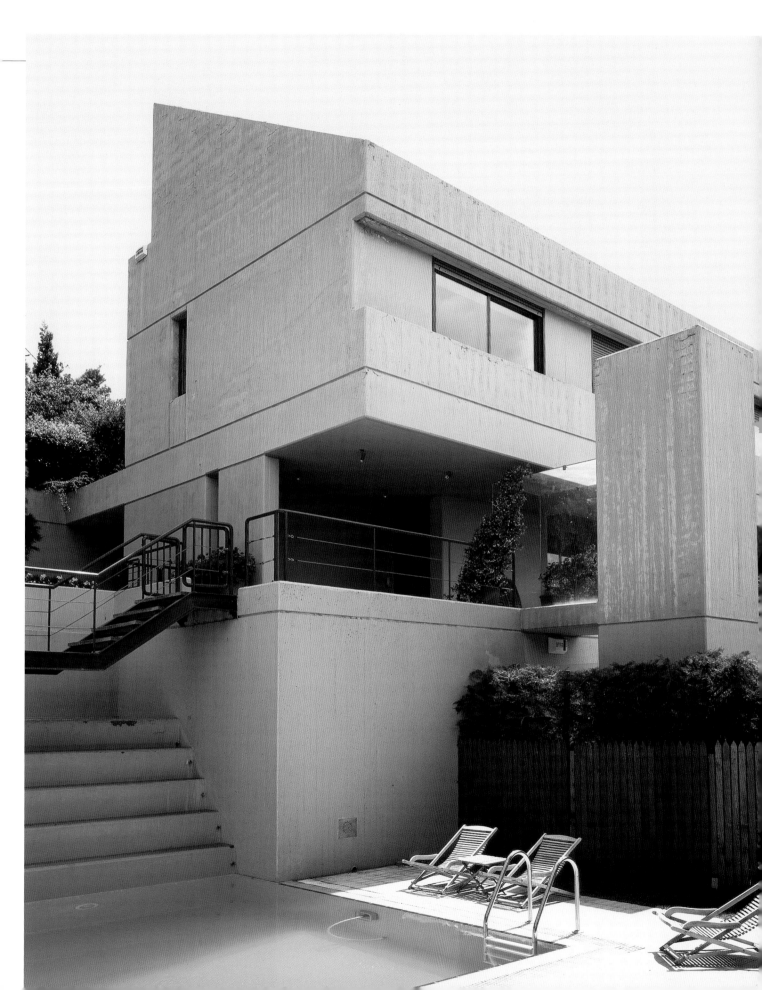

Above: **Sofianos House, Athens, Greece.** The doors and door fittings, as well as the windows and radiators, were all detailed in a red finish made possible by the availability in the 1970s of standardised colours, and products like the Modric door handles and escutcheons that were self-coloured in fashionable hues.

The second most significant space of the house is the L-shaped living–dining room. The long part of the L runs from the front to the back of the house and is a double-height space at its centre as it is open to the roof on the atrium side. On the end wall of the house and beneath the apex of the roof is a tall chimney breast, which terminates at an unsupported canopy above a wide fireplace sitting on a timber-faced plinth that runs, cantilevered, the full length of the atrium side of the dining–living area. The rear of the room overlooking the boscage has a low range of windows running its length. Unlike the atrium the room has a conventional ceiling. Throughout the house the floors are of warm-toned, narrow-strip timber and the walls are white. Everywhere the walls are covered by the owners' ever-growing collection of contemporary art lit by the original tracklights. The front end of the living room is a library area and this joins the dining area, which also faces the front. These give access onto the veranda through red-framed double-glazed picture windows with built-in electric shutters constructed of Iroko.

From the dining room there is an entrance to a large fitted kitchen and the service rooms beyond. Like all the fitted furniture in the bedrooms and other service rooms, the kitchen units were specially manufactured to a Tombazis design and are faced in pale grey. Door furniture is in red nylon to match the window frames used throughout the house. The bathrooms and cloakroom pick up the use of primary colours and the use of nylon door furniture and are typical of architect-designed bathroom areas in the 1970s. This is particularly true of the cloakroom, which is a top-lit room lined throughout in square tiles grouted to match the basin and its fittings, which are made of various plastics coloured a primary yellow. The large fitted mirror above the basin is also a common 1970s design feature that was used to increase the apparent size of small enclosed rooms.

The bedrooms are ranged along the upper storey and look out across the valley to the mountains beyond through sliding ribbon windows finished in red. The interiors of the rooms are open to the pitched roof, a vernacular feature in Greece, and in addition are lit by thin clerestory windows in the top of the rear wall just below the joint with the roof.

The combined effect of the use of an almost collegiate plan of the rooms, their plain walls, grey fitted furniture and red-finished industrial windows, together with the very simple inexpressive exterior form and finishes gives the building a utilitarianism that recalls some British public building of the late 1970s. The architect's use of industrial-looking fittings, harsh non-domestic colours and basic forms in concrete contrast with the lushness of the atrium–boscage area, which is invisible to the outside world, and the scale, restrained chic and comfort of the living area. But the greatest contrast in the design is between the bare street elevation of the house and the swimming pool that lies in the lower garden. Though there is now a freestanding exterior lift down to the pool, a drop of 3 metres, the original design was no less conspicuously expensive. The side of the pool cut into the hillside is a stepped waterfall, and access to the pool is by a wood and stainless-steel bridge and stairway that crosses this cascade on its way to the pool edge.

This house reflects the ambivalence of some late 1970s architecture. It seems to be striving for sustainability in its use of solar heat, off-the-shelf building materials and artless planning, but this contrasts wildly with the unecological treatment of the site, which was blasted from virgin hillside, and the excessively consumptive pool, not to mention the latter's over-the-top means of access. This combination of ecosensitivity with an equal lack of moderation reflects the conflict between the client's desire for the freedom to consume as an individual and the architect's emerging concern about the effects of unfettered consumption on society as a whole.

Above: **Sofianos House, Athens, Greece.** By the later 1970s there was a whole infrastructure of manu-facturers of stylish fittings, all of whom produced designs within an aesthetic that celebrated machine manufacture and synthetic material and colours. This led to an, in retrospect, limited range of styles and fittings, which were used again and again by architects everywhere. At the Sofianos House, Tombazis used this standard vocabulary in his Italian-inspired guest washroom, combining a very conventional arrangement of mirrors and top-lighting with a more radical fibreglass hand basin.

Opposite: **Sofianos House, Athens, Greece.** The Sofianos House was Tombazis' first exercise in passive climate control, achieved by the circulation of air through the building, which is built into a steep rock hillside. The atrium differs from later 1980s and 1990s atria by being open to the elements. In an area where temperatures can reach 40°C, it is protected from overheating by shade from the steep hillside and from a plane tree in the courtyard. The combination of courtyard and plane tree is part of the basic language of Greek exterior space and, combined with the pool, is typical of the dichotomies of Athenian society.

Sametz House

Alfredo De Vido

Garrison, New York, USA   1979   1972-74

Garrison lies on the east bank of the Hudson River across from West Point. Although easily accessible from Manhattan via the Hudson Parkway, the area is far less built up than Long Island, even though it also has its fair share of grand houses from the 19th and early 20th centuries. The Sametz House lies in woods in the grounds of a large late 19th-century house with few other houses nearby. The chief virtue of the site, apart from discretion, is the stunning views it provides of the Hudson River. These recall the paintings of the Hudson River School, in particular the view upriver, which has a sublime grandeur. Once New York is left behind the Hudson flows through a wide gorge, flanked by wooded hills on both sides up to West Point, where its escarped channel suddenly opens out into a wider and seemingly unlimited landscape under a vast sky. This is the view from the Sametz House.

In contrast to the habits of developers in the 1980s and 1990s, although the house stands in 2 acres it is small, being essentially a 30-foot cube built of stained-cedar siding attached to a wooden frame, with hardwood floors and interior walls of 'sheetrock'. Like many American houses its construction is pragmatic and uses techniques and materials that are well understood by local craftsmen. The wooden construction is light, strong, flexible and surprisingly durable, and this simplicity and reliability permitted the architect to allow himself to design according to primarily formal criteria relatively unrestricted by material limitations.

This is evident on the exteriors where the cubic module is used to unify the whole, meaning that the verandas and the pitched roofs are contained within a thin wooden facade. The architect used the difference between the apparent volume of the house and the actual layout of the interior forms to create voids in the exterior facade that play with our conventional expectations of support and mass. This is particularly evident in the principal river-view elevation of the house and the entrance elevation. In both, voids are made at the corners of the cube creating a sense of lightness in the structure, which contrasts with the black-stained siding. Surprisingly, the blackness of the exterior keys in well with the trunks of the trees in the dense woodland surrounding the house on three sides, and also emphasises the lightness of the white interior, which is clearly visible through uncurtained windows.

The layout of the interior reflects the weekend–holiday function of the house and combines established architectural styles from Long Island with Corbusian features that recall his Pavilion de l'Esprit Nouveau of 1925.

The residence is a tower house laid out according to a hierarchy of use. From a carport a small stairway leads to an entrance hall, which is practically

Sametz House, New York, USA. Although more often seen in natural or white, De Vido here used black siding for his design. This contrasts with the voids in the facade and the white-painted interior behind the fenestration, and the resulting mixture of neutral but contrasting forms seems to help dematerialise the presence of the house in the wooded landscape. The form of the house is a well-established vernacular in north-eastern America, derived from a style of weekend house developed in the flat landscape of Long Island in the mid-1960s. The style took advantage of the potential of wood construction to allow the erection of light buildings in which openings could be placed at any point. This gave architects the opportunity to give their structures the kind of abstract formal purity seen in post-war American painting and European Modernist architectonics.

Above: **Sametz House, New York, USA.**
Despite the apparent spaciousness of the Sametz House the central space is actually very restricted by stairways and doors.

Opposite: **Sametz House, New York, USA.**
The chief purpose of the Sametz House is as a weekend retreat from the rigours of Manhattan life. A major part of this escape is the sense of unbounded space and the sublime majesty of the American landscape. This is provided here by the magnificent view of the Hudson valley and the promise of the unfolding continent beyond the gap at West Point, which can be seen from many parts of the house

laid out to suit its role as what used to be called a boot room. From here there is access to a rather functional bedroom with a double aspect, from which stairs lead up to another small bedroom and a guest bathroom on a half-landing, and then up again to the *piano nobile* of the house. Here, the stairs enter a double-height living space fenestrated on three sides, of which two – facing north and north-west – have picture windows topped by clerestory lights. The room also has skylights above its southern end which, unlike the rest of the room, doesn't have full-height wall glazing. This is to allow space for built-in seating below shortened windows. The room faces north-west and lies next to a veranda, accessed via picture windows, that also faces the principal view and looks north.

On the south wall, next to the stairs, is a wood fire open on two sides and this lies adjacent to the entrance to the southeast-facing kitchen. Surprisingly, the simple fitted kitchen is separate from the living area, despite the layout of the upper floors being otherwise very Corbusian with its double-height living space created by the use of a mezzanine floor all lit by double-height windows. On a half-landing above the living area there is a large library–study–bedroom with a small balcony, linked to the living-room veranda by a short stairway, from which it too shares the principal view. The study has full-height fenestration on two sides, and the library area – which lies behind the stairwell on the south side of the house – is lit by a large north-facing skylight, thus freeing up the walls for books. The study–library room is a one-and-a-half-height space and shares its ceiling with the double-height living area and the single-height master bedroom that occupies a mezzanine projecting into the living room. This is reached by a half-stair from the study–library half-landing. The top bedroom has a double aspect to the south and west. To the rear of the master bedroom and above the kitchen is an en-suite bathroom. The colour scheme throughout is white walls, hardwood floors and pine ceilings, with the exception of the stairs and kitchen floor which are covered with terracotta tiles.

The design of the house is effectively divided into two; a lower area that contains services, storage and guest accommodation and an upper house proper for the principal occupants. This upper house uses the shared ceiling height and linked verandas to unify a complex multilayered space that is indebted to Le Corbusier's 1920s house designs and his recognition that height imbues even small areas with a sense of luxury. In fact, the house is a late example of a local Modernist vernacular that goes back to the mid-1960s

Above: Sametz House, New York, USA.
American houses could rely on modern technology long before their counterparts in Europe. The
thinness of the walls, the vast open spaces and
the equally vast areas of uncurtained glazing in
the Sametz House are only practicable because
of superior insulation and heating technology.
Leaving aside the efficient insulating qualities of
the wood, the house benefits from positive hot-air
heating, double-glazing and cavity-wall insulation.
These discreet technologies allowed the architect
to enhance the spaciousness of the house, using
Corbusian heights to the principal rooms and
devices like extended windows in the bedroom.

Right: Sametz House, New York, USA.
One effect of the long-established formula for
standardising kitchens and bathrooms was that
these could be treated as if they were white-
goods units in their own right, like fridges. This
approach has tended to disappear since the
1970s, as these rooms became another area for
the expression of individual taste and culture

designs of Long Island weekend houses, developed around the idea of tall houses, to facilitate views that are maximised by the use of levels, rather than distinct floors, and that offer different and, where possible, double aspects. In this house these levels are articulated around half-landings on the staircase. On the upper level of the house this is used to create a sense of three interlinked floors within one double-height space. Given this Corbusian treatment of the principal spaces, it is surprising that both the kitchen and en-suite bathroom are completely separated from the areas that they serve. Equally idiosyncratic is the separation of the guest rooms from the main body of the house, although this is a habit of design that dominates the architecture of weekend retreats and reflects the ambivalence of the relationship between owners and guests.

Above and right: **Sametz House, New York, USA.** With such a small living area, it is perhaps surprising that the fireplace is placed in its crowded centre. However, this allows uninterrupted views and an alternative and comforting focus at the heart of the house. Although the fire is open on two sides in a very unconventional manner, it actually provides a central point that unifies the L-shaped room at its apex, which adds to the overall sense of spaciousness in the house.

AUTO-
ARCHITECTURAL

In considering any architectural design there is always the question of the effect of the relationship between the architect and the client, and various other pragmatic considerations beyond the architect's control, such as the nature of the site, its context and the adjudications of the local planning committee. If it were possible to show buildings where the architect had almost total control over all aspects of their production, this would at least give an indication of true architects' architecture. In a brief survey like this, which is attempting to describe neither a movement nor an architect's *oeuvre* but the changes of a decade, some account of architecture built for the architects themselves should help to indicate their aesthetic position more clearly than houses built on behalf of others, which are necessarily, therefore, more compromised designs.

Autoarchitectural

The houses featured in this section are all designed by the architects for their own use. They can be seen as a pure expression of the architecture that architects wanted at the time of their construction, the 1970s. All the examples discussed here were built when the architects could first afford to build for themselves and are therefore expressions of an accumulation of ideas about what architecture should be rather than what it can be. Finally, all the houses are still owned and used by the architects and their families, and so may be judged to be successful self-expressions.

A great attraction for the documentarist of these houses is that, being self-designed and still used by the families they were built for, the buildings are a kind of time capsule of the lifestyle desires of the architects at a particular point in their development. They represent a kind of essential 'seventiesness' that reveals the social context of architecture that underlies the particular design synthesis of the architect. In short, the architecture that architects built for themselves reflects the architectural *Zeitgeist* of the time.

The 1970s was a period that still favoured internationalism and the idea of universal solutions to individual problems where the concept of an international architectural *Zeitgeist* retained a currency that it would be unable to claim today with our concern for the local and the individual. However, the 1970s was also the period where the universalising Modernism of the post-war years was beginning to be challenged by wide-ranging critiques of cultural assumptions. These were shared across many professions, for example, in books like E F Schumacher's (1973) *Small is Beautiful: Study of Economics as if People Mattered*. Critiques that related to architectural practice were not restricted to the revisionist attacks on Modernism by Venturi, Rossi and Jencks but also came in the form of the ecological challenge of Victor Papanek's (1972) *Design for the Real World: Human Ecology and Social Change.* There was also the frequent suggestion that architecture would be replaced by consumer technology, as in Banham and Dallegret's 1965 article on 'The Unhouse'.[1]

For much of the decade these challenges, pertinent to architecture as they were, represented symptoms of a deep cultural change rather than effecting change in themselves. At the level of architectural practice it is only possible to say that there was a general recognition that one size does not fit all, and this resulted in an increase in experimentation by architects. The buildings in this section do, in some way, express challenges to the architectural dogma of the 1960s, which in itself was a continuation of many ideas that were developed in earlier decades.

Some of these ideas were no more than assumptions given architectural form based on common-sense attitudes in society, for instance the situation of children or the relationship between work and home. It was perceived societal norms, such as these, that were the focus of the sociological critique of society that developed in the 1960s and 1970s. Following the lead of critical theorists from other disciplines, architecture in the 1970s tried to respond to this changing intellectual culture by developing designs that responded to these critiques, some of which find expression in the examples discussed here.

At the same time architectural discourse began to reconsider its own shibboleths, not least its relationship with architectures that were outside the architectural rationale, still dominant in the mid-1970s, to create, 'new architecture which is a simple and unselfconscious expression of present-day requirements'.[2] These included architectural traditions of non-European countries, vernacular architecture, ecological architecture and socially flexible architecture. The result of all these challenges to the professional orthodoxies of the late 1960s and early 1970s was an increasing eclecticism among architects. Over the decade they began to explore their discipline and its traditions beyond the boundaries of their Modernist training but, as is evident from the buildings discussed here, in general they worked without any concern as to their position in respect of the fundamental motivations of architecture; rather, in this case they tried to use their skills to give themselves the environments that they wanted.

Josef Paul Kleihues' Kleines Atelier addresses the problem of work–life balance. Although the building is much more of a workplace than a living place its site in the garden of his home, directly adjacent to the side door of the main family house, shows that the architect wished in some way to unify his home and work and achieved this by creating a hybrid office-cum-house close to his family. The remarkable thing about this space is its intense masculinity, so that although it says one thing by its proximity to the family its actual form is a very assertive statement about the nature of the office and its incompatibility with 'home' life. This dualism or dichotomy, between what is expressed in the setting and what is expressed in the form, is emblematic of the unresolved nature of architecture in the 1970s.

This tendency towards what Jencks would call multivalent architecture that is more in the nature of an unresolved position than self-conscious eclecticism, is also apparent in the De Vido House. In this case there is no question that it is a home, despite the presence of a studio in the grounds, because here it is the language of leisure rather than work–home that

BY SUSAN ZEVON   PHOTOGRAPHY BY JUDITH WATTS

De Vido House, Long Island, USA. Al De Vido's design for his own house – shown here in an article for *Architectural Record* of May 1969 – reflects an interest in the traditional American timber architecture of barns which, in contrast to the domestic vernacular of 'salt-box' cottages, provided the kind of large spaces that suited late 20th century tastes.

House and family grow together

"I just can't keep my hands off it," says architect Alfredo De Vido about his summer place

1 | 2

dominates throughout. The complexity in this case is in the relation of the whole to the different traditions of America, Scandinavia and Japan from which the house is synthesised. The De Vido House is indicative of the search among architects for a way out of the narrow language of domestic Modernism that might express more eloquently the complex meanings that the home has.

By contrast, Casa Marti is an apparently simple approach to the same problem. It embraces the many ideas of the home holistically by adopting a matrix through which the diversity of these meanings can be explored. In solving the issue of what the home means to his family, by creating a space where it may mean anything at any time, Marti has come up with a design that touches on other issues for 1970s architects. Foremost among these are possibility and flexibility, and his design shares similar concerns and concepts with Piano and Rogers' Centre Pompidou in Paris. In essence, Casa Marti is a frame for living that can be adapted and reconfigured to accommodate the needs of the occupants using materials that can be modelled and deployed by the family itself. This individualism is also an element that was important in the 1970s, and Casa Marti represents the highly informal, communitarian and low-tech architectural movement, which has continuously acted as a critique to the conservative drift of the architectural profession since then.

The Tombazis House, though designed in the context of issues similar to those affecting Casa Marti, is concerned with different aspects of what in that period was considered an 'alternative' political position. Tombazis' concern is with energy conservation and what were called children's rights more than with the general idea of freedom that forms Casa Marti. Tombazis addresses these by using the long-established Modernist practice of solving problems individually, as if they were engineering problems, through carefully considered detailing applied to simple and well-established domestic forms. In his design, a traditional Modernist open-planned L is adapted to the emergent green technology and design practices by being set in the earth and by the use of solar panels. Equally Modernist is the way that the tower on the house, an unusual change to the original Modernist L, solves the design 'problems' of how best to use the solar panels and create a 'child-centred' environment.

The Tombazis House demonstrates the necessity of changing the Modernist practices of the 1960s, a situation that was brought about by technical and social Modernism developing faster than architecture could. Inasmuch as the house was conceived and executed as a conventional Modernist home, its development was altered by developments that were equally Modernist yet emerged from areas that were formerly beyond the scope of the architect's responsibility – technology and sociology. It was the progressive and idealist tendency in Modernist architecture – to try constantly to act as a good forward-looking citizen – that led architects of the 1970s to the position where they were heading into more complex architectural conditions, by choice but without a programme. This state of being is analogous to Jean-Francois Lyotard's summary of the conditions that arise in the transition from one epistemological paradigm to another, in this case the transition from Modernism to where we are now.

1   Reyner Banham and Francois Dallegret, 'The Unhouse', *Art In America*, April 1965.

2   Bertrand de Jouvenel, *The Art of Conjecture*, Basic Books (London),1967, p 284. Quoted in Charles Jencks, *Modern Movements in Architecture*, Penguin Books Ltd (Harmondsworth),1973, p 76.

Modric Door Furniture. Though originally produced in 1965, when it received a Council of Industrial Design (CoID) award, Alan Tye's Modric range became most popular in the 1970s, when it was made in a variety of finishes and colours in aluminium, steel or plastic. The great achievement of the range was the reliable matching of the wide range of components, both in form and finish, despite the variety of manufacturing processes that were used to create its various elements.

Kleines Atelier

Josef Paul Kleihues
Schlachtensee, Berlin, Germany   1968-74

Josef Paul Kleihues, who recently died, was one of the major public architects of Berlin from the 1960s to the 1990s. He made his home in the Wilhelmine suburb of Schlachtensee, which has an arboreal pleasantness unique to Berlin. The Schlachtensee is a small, landlocked lake in the district of Zehlendorf on the way to Potsdam, on the edge of the Grunewald, a forest-cum-park long used as a sort of Bois de Boulogne by Berliners. The Kleihues Atelier lies on a small hill a few minutes walk from the well-wooded hollow of the lake, with its boating and swimming. Shopping and the S-Bahn are minutes away, at the perfect Landhausstil Mexicoplatz with its aura of imperial certainty.

The main house has a similar air of 1900s solidity, being in the rather severe style of simplified Neoclassicism that was favoured by Behrens and featured in the early work of Mies van der Rohe during the first years of the 20th century. The subsequent restoration of the house has, if anything, made this style more severe. In the late 1960s the architect decided to build an *atelier* in the garden of his house. The term implies a studio, but the building is actually a small, self-contained house made up of two ranges. In the principal range the space is given over to a large living area and studio, from which there is access to the subsidiary second range. This contains a washroom, kitchen and bedroom to the rear, and a garage at the front.

The two ranges are laid out side by side and run the full depth of the main house, from which they are separated by a cobbled pathway. The range nearest the main house forms the studio, with full-height, full-width steel-framed glazing to the front and rear, while the blank side walls are lit from sloping skylights that run the whole length of the room between the walls and the roof at an angle of 45 degrees. The second range is about a metre lower than the principal range and has a full-width, slab-like ceiling. The only windows in this range are skylights for the centrally located galley kitchen and equally small washroom, and full-height steel-framed windows in the double bedroom. The bedroom and the rear windows of the studio overlook an apple tree, framed by a semicircular wall the width of both ranges. This has the spatial effect of terminating the view and helping to establish the sense that the Kleines Atelier is a distinct and separate entity from the house that overshadows it. This is also suggested by a course of bricks that runs in the grass from the end of the studio to 'its' garden wall. The studio is entered by a double door that faces a corresponding secondary entrance to the main house. Directly opposite the studio entrance doors is a double-width lobby that gives access to the bedroom, the galley kitchen and the washroom.

Above: **Kleines Atelier, Berlin, Germany.** The detailing of the passage between the family house and the studio is deliberately understated. A steel grid running from the double-width side exit of the main house to the double-width entrance to the studio opposite links the buildings. The cobbles of the dividing passage, and other features like the light at the front, create a unifying textural vista between the two external walls.

Opposite and top right: **Kleines Atelier, Berlin, Germany.** Although made up of two ranges, the Kleines Atelier building is designed to appear primarily as though it were only one. This is achieved through the device of having the central bay of the studio projecting forwards and above the rest of the structure, and presenting the front end of the second range as a garage, which is also obscured by planting. The Brutalist style is achieved by using the visual language of engineering structures. There are no cross walls below the concrete slab that forms the roof and this, combined with the concrete cornice to the semi-engineering brick walls, creates the impression of a bridge-like structure. However, there are other details that unify the building with its context. The most discreet is the single course of bricks set in the grass and terminating in a semi-circular wall that defines the studio's portion of the garden, which includes the domesticating presence of an apple tree.

The atelier is built from dark engineering brick, while the metal-framed windows and doors are painted black and the floor is black thermoplastic. The walls of the atelier are freestanding, while the roof is supported by slab-like pilasters of brick. The external walls and the pilasters are topped with concrete capitals. Mounted on panels supported by thin spotlight batons attached to the ceiling in the gaps between the pilasters are spotlights, facing both the centre of the room and the walls. The studio is divided into two spaces. A sitting area with high-backed black sofas and a pair of matching black coffee tables is located at the garden end, with a long work desk filling the remaining two thirds of the space. At the 'studio end' of the atelier is a mixture of pre-computer drawing office equipment and an old-fashioned stereo system. The kitchen has a prefabricated cooker–fridge unit and some built-in storage, both of which are white. The washroom and the kitchen are top-lit by circular, vacuum-moulded skylights. The windows are fitted with foil blinds. The roof lights are of wired glass.

The whole is an essay in Brutalist styling, using a similar language of concrete, brick and industrial fittings and details that is found in parts of the Barbican in London. Given the severe restraint of the white stuccoed main house, the Brutalism of the atelier seems entirely appropriate, even sympathetic.

The Kleihues Atelier is an unusual domestic building because it is overwhelmingly and uncompromisingly masculine. The extreme severity of the architecture, the very deliberate dark simplicity, the use of hard materials,

Kleines Atelier, Berlin, Germany. The engineering Brutalism of the exterior gives the interior the feel of an industrial unit, and this is enhanced by the self-consciously industrial pragmatism of the design of the spotlights. The glazing of the studio gives a good even light, and the layout of the centrally placed work area is free from the distractions of views from the end windows. The working interior is representative of the pre-CAD office, with its drawing desks, Anglepoise lamps, plan chests, fax and photocopier.

bare lamps, shiny surfaces and minimal services all represent a very male disregard for obvious comfort beyond the minimal. Equally, the fetishisation of work – big desks, plan chests and the paraphernalia of the office displaying a love of technological pleasures – together with the reification of the stereo system distinguishes this building as a male preserve and separates it from the domesticity of the adjacent house. In a sense the siting of the studio suggests an attempt to soften the separation of work and home in line with the more progressive thinking of the day, whereas the architecture and interior furnishings of the atelier suggest quite the reverse.

The 1970s Brutalism that articulates the atelier is the acme of architectural masculinism, and is far more assertive and gendered than the domestic architecture of the 1960s. Moreover, it prefigures the unchallenged masculinism of the technically and theoretically driven architectural styles of the 1980s and 1990s. What in the 1960s would have been configured as an artists studio, though retaining the term *atelier*, is in fact a new kind of space that we now take for granted – the live–work space – except that here living and working become conflated, and the atelier brings the masculine refuge of the office closer to the home.

In many ways the Kleines Atelier seems the most obvious evidence of a reaction against the often noted feminisation of culture during the 1960s, in favour of something that rebels against the idea of turning our lives toward leisure, and instead reconfigures real leisure as work. The main aesthetic work of this building is to make work sexy. In fact the building resembles an office block in the garden more than a studio.

Casa Marti

Sep Marti
Solduno, Valle Maggia, Ticino, Switzerland 1976

Lake Maggiore takes its name from the Maggia River. They meet at Locarno where the Maggia's pristine waters refresh the tired lake. So clean and powerful is its spring flow that its bed of sparkling white granite and green marble is always clean. In summer it is gentle enough to make the river a lido for local children. As the Maggia curves down from the mountains the inner curves have become small suburban plains, and on the outer curves the steeply cut valleys are filled with hanging homes. On the steep bank at Solduno, just outside Locarno, the river's edge is crowded by the road and railway up the valley, so much so that, from either, the Maggia is only visible behind occasional rows of parked cars. Yet between the road and the river are yet more homes, clinging onto the wooded river edge. This is the site of Casa Marti – the house that Sep Marti built for his family. Remarkably, it manages to be secluded among trees despite the proximity of Locarno's outer suburbs. Marti, who has run a modest practice since 1961, first in Bad Ragaz and then in Zurich, is known internationally only on the basis of his house. It is featured in the literature of Ticino architecture, and also in magazines like *Architectural Review* for which it was photographed by Richard Einzig in 1977.

To exist at all the house sits on an L-shaped foundation of concrete that both supports it and protects it from the road's embankment. So cramped is the site that the roof is also the car park for the house, making the building completely invisible from the road. The form of the house is simple. A concrete frame, like a 3-D noughts-and-crosses game, contains a large space entered at the mid level. Beyond the frame is a further frame of pink tubular steel. The two frames are joined by a precipitous veranda of steel grids. On the three vertical faces overlooking the river the cells created by the structure are filled with plate glass. To the rear a breeze-block wall defines the back of the main house and makes space for a studio, for the family's creative endeavours, between the concrete retaining wall and the back of the house. Inside the main house the space is presently divided into four upper rooms, a large double-height living–cooking area and a bathroom with a hot tub overlooking the river. The top floor is made up of three rooms, while one cell of the double-height lower level is floored over and balustraded to make a study area. The rest of the main body of the house is living space, with the bathroom in a ground-floor room attached to the exterior of the main frame of the building. Stairs and corridors run along the back wall of the house.

A jungly path leads down from the road to a small bridge over the gap between the foundation frame and the body of the house and then there is a 90-degree turn into the house on the first floor from a top-lit entrance area.

Above: **Casa Marti, Ticino, Switzerland.** The tiled floor of the living area is a recent addition; the original floor was concrete painted in lilac and pink circular forms.

Opposite: **Casa Marti, Ticino, Switzerland.** The steel Rubik's cube of the house, its sylvan riverine setting and Floridian colour scheme all express the essence of Casa Marti, where the simple, logical frame provides a freedom for its owners to lay out the interior as they please. In the background can be seen the overhead cables of the railway line, which runs next to the road that passes by the rear of the house. Clever siting and construction create a sense of isolation in what is in fact a suburb of Locarno.

Above: Casa Marti, Ticino, Switzerland. The house is entered from the side, at the first floor level, where there is an open gallery *(see page 93)*, with stairs leading up to the bedrooms or down to the living and bathing areas. The narrow, vertiginous stairs are movable units designed and made by the architect. The pink plywood swing in the entrance gallery is as much part of the language of the design as the small, square-section timbers that are loosely laid to form the upper floors of the building.

Opposite: Casa Marti, Ticino, Switzerland. The original ceiling height in the main living space was five metres, but as the use of the building grew to incorporate studios, studies and more bedrooms the upper level of the open space was floored over. The original central light fitting and dining table and chairs remain in the room, but in the kitchen the original cooking–eating area has been altered from a communal low-level arrangement to one of standing height as the owners have grown older.

The effect of this convoluted and bosky entry is to give a sense of dislocation from the suburban road above. It succeeds not least because the wooded riverine setting of this glass box fills the house with a complex variety of natural light giving the impression of a remote rather than rural setting. The interior was designed to offer the maximum flexibility to its owners, rather like a mini Centre Pompidou. Looking up from the living area to the floors above, it is immediately apparent that they are made of assorted, light, densely packed timber pieces cut to length and upon which the floor's surface sits. The walls upstairs are made from exterior-quality plywood, and the sliding panels that serve as closures for the rooms are made of the same material.

This use of cheap, low-specification building materials is a fundamental behind the design, as is interchangeability which is strikingly represented by the steep, movable stair units that rise through the house. The architect not only used cheap readily available materials, where possible, he also used local labour. There are some very ingenious bits of Adhocism in the house, such as the use of sections of concrete drainage pipes of various widths for washbasins and the large hot tub on the ground floor. The architect also created some unique designs for his living space, like the high-backed and low-seated dining chairs in white-painted wood and the spectacular cooking–eating area. Originally this was made up of a stove and cooking range built into a freestanding plinth that was set low to the floor so that guests or family could sit around this warm area next to where the food was being prepared by someone also sitting down. Over the years this system became impractical and the whole arrangement is now at standing height. When the house was first finished the floor of the ground level was painted in a predominantly mauve pattern but the paint's lack of durability eventually led to this floor being tiled. Other changes reflecting the architect's green outlook were the fitting of solar panels to the roof (the only other heating in the house is from a wood-fired stove) and improvements to the glazing arrangements as the old windows began to fail.

Casa Marti was created by the architect for his family's needs, and built from cheap, low-impact materials and technologies yet with great elegance and clarity of design. It shows that the best architecture of the 1970s had moved towards a liberated, flexible architecture driven by the needs of the individual and a regard for ecological issues. At the same time architects had also moved away from the bungalow tendency of the Modernist individual home towards designs that functioned in three dimensions rather than as sequences of rooms.

Opposite: **Casa Marti, Ticino, Switzerland.** The studio space is a wooden structure added to the house at a later date. It is used by the whole family and reflects their differing and changing interests. The architect's emphasis on creating flexible space, exemplified here by the sound-room constructed within the double-height studio, has enabled the family to grow and change within the envelope of the original site at minimal cost and effort, which in itself encourages creative exploration.

Below: **Casa Marti, Ticino, Switzerland.** The bathroom is in an extension, constructed from breeze blocks, to the side of the house, which also enabled an extension to the studio space above. The washbasins and hot tub are made from concrete sections of drainage pipes that were then painted or tiled in common with the low-tech Adhocism of the rest of the house.

Above: **Casa Marti, Ticino, Switzerland.** Much of the interior of this room was made within the Marti home and is an expression of the mildly counter-cultural ethos of self-build that evolved in the late 1960s and was popular until the late 1970s. The use of natural-hued, highly textured materials is also typical of the period. The wall to the room and the shelving are both made from sawn wood and exterior-grade plywood sheet available from builders' merchants, and cheap semi-industrial materials are used to advantage throughout the house. The pink steel exterior frame gives access to the windows for cleaning and repair purposes, and is made from easily available steel tubing and gratings.

Tombazis House

Alexandros Tombazis

Trapeza Aigialeias, Patras, Greece   1977

At weekends, at Easter and in August it is traditional in Athens, as in many overcrowded capitals, for anyone who is able to leave the city to do so. Unlike in most of Europe the countryside near Athens is relatively empty and very close to the Mediterranean, and thus it is ideal for weekend and holiday retreats. The surprise is that relatively few new homes are built outside Athens. This is because of the tradition of returning to one's own village, originally abandoned for a better life in Athens, where the family homestead has usually been retained as a second home. The Tombazis family were unusual in buying a new piece of land for a summer home, and this gave them the freedom to pick a site that related to the landscape and the view rather than the settlement of the nearby village of Trapeza Aigialeias near Patras. The land is on a hillside that runs down towards the Gulf of Corinth and looks out across the sea towards Mount Parnassus and the ancient site of Delphi in the foothills below. Set beneath its own range of beautiful mountains and surrounded by groves of fruit trees and vineyards, Tombazis House, Helios 1, is also convenient for the main road and railway to Athens making it an ideal retreat. The name of the house reflects its special status as the first solar-heated house in Greece.

The site of Helios 1 reflects Tombazis' concern to develop a more ecologically aware architecture and, as has since become a standard practice for green buildings, most of the house is set in the hillside to moderate the temperature within. However, although he has built his practice on an ecological foundation, Tombazis is not primarily a domestic architect; rather, most of his output has been a mixture of public buildings, religious institutions and corporate offices.

The plan of the house is a conventional Modernist L, and it is the internal aspect of the L that forms the exposed facades of the house; the rest is set into the hillside. Most of the building is laid out as a bungalow with the exception of a tower for the children's bedrooms, which would otherwise have had no view. On the outside of the tower, on its inland south face, are located the solar panels that heat the domestic water supply and the radiators. The space at the centre of the L has been made into a patio or external room, and in summer this is where most of the family's time is spent. The external patio and the internal areas of the house can be unified into one

Above: **Tombazis House, Patras, Greece.** This house was the first one in Greece to be designed with solar panels and, as their aesthetic treatment had no established language, the architect has borrowed from the lexicon of rooflights to articulate these new technical features. Tombazis has further made a virtue of necessity by using the panel module inside for the living-area roof. This is treated as the inverse of the external panels, including the reversal of their colour so that inside the roof is white whereas elsewhere in the house it is natural timber.

Opposite: **Tombazis House, Patras, Greece.** Because the house is mostly on one storey set into the ground, the roofscape has become the principal facade. This is treated as a series of Brutalist abstract sculptures in a garden. The almost geological effect of the texture and colours of the lead facings of the roof of the master suite and the children's tower is enhanced by the loose rocks that cover the master-suite roof and the shape of the tower, all of which, the architect has said, relates to the mountains behind.

Tombazis House, Patras, Greece. The patio was conceived as the centre of the house onto which the majority of the rooms lead, and all the rooms look towards the sea with their backs to the hillside. The site and layout of the house are all elements that feature in the house plans of Greek settlements back to the Mycenaean period. Equally, in many respects the house is typical of the conventional Modernist bungalow, and the modern architect's aspiration to unite interior and exterior space is fully realised in this design, not only through the patio but also through the covered areas that give protection from the fierce sun.

truly open-plan living space by the retracting full-height windows, which open in such a manner as to leave no trace of glazing or framing at the internal angle of the house. In addition, the fireplace in the living area is mirrored on the outside by an external fireplace below the other vertical feature of the house – a substantial brick chimney, the top of which reflects the wedge form of the solar-panel tower. Both of these features are faced with lead. Inside, the kitchen–dining–living area is on a split level that follows the contours of the site, and the lower level, below the dining area, forms a sunken sitting 'pool' that has its own view of the sea. This is not shared by the kitchen–dining area, which looks inwards to the patio.

Outside, the patio ends in a drop to another lower level, which is terminated to the west by a veranda in front of the living area. This complex combination of internal and external areas at various levels and exposures is designed so that every aspect of the weather is catered for. The spaces are disposed about the site in such a way as to make it impossible not to fully use all the space on offer, thus maximising the use of the 80 x 80-metre site. The structure of the house is a mixture of concrete, for the retaining walls, and brick, for the chimney and other visible walls, combined with a redwood pine timber frame which is either left exposed (inside) or sheathed in lead (outside). The patio is of concrete divided into brick-edged panels and the ground floor is quarry tiled. The internal walls are clad in tongue-and-groove pine laid horizontally, and the kitchen units are faced in flush-finished pine with a white Formica worktop. Internal doors are flush panelled and finished in light olive green. Throughout, the door furniture and other fittings are red nylon except those of the Barbican-style picture windows, which are aluminium.

The bedrooms are laid out so that the master bedroom is reached by a short corridor facing the patio. At the back of the bedroom is an *en-suite* bathroom lit by a vacuum-moulded plastic skylight. Leading off the same corridor is the second bathroom, also lit by a skylight. The children's rooms are reached by two separate and compact pine ladders rising behind the kitchen in a sky-lit extension of the patio corridor. Between the ladders is more storage. The children's rooms are a rare example of a child-friendly design that follows the most radical of 1970s ideas – that children have a right to their own space designed to be fun and free of adults. Once attained, they open out into double-height spaces illuminated by long, thin side windows on the external end walls of the rooms, and by large, round, vacuum-moulded plastic windows facing the sea. These are set above bunk beds, which are built high on the walls and accessed by a series of red plastic climbing handles set into the bookshelves that line the wall separating the two rooms. On the back walls are two further bunks, and below the long end windows are built-in Formica-topped desks. Both rooms are lined with horizontal tongue-and-groove pine.

In contrast to the established architectural practice of locating both children's and guests' rooms in remote parts of the house, Tombazis followed a more sociologically informed architectural practice. He gave his children rooms that were simultaneously at the centre of the home, a clamber away from food, big enough to allow two guests per child and inaccessible to all but the most committed adults. This enlightened attitude emerged in the 1970s, but has since disappeared as a result of the passive safety culture of current design for children and the resurgent self-centredness of adults concerned with their own comfort.

Tombazis House, Patras, Greece. The kitchen, dining and living areas follow the popular split-level formula with the kitchen and dining at the top and the sitting area in a well that is vertically spacious but has a small floor area that focuses on the fire making it a cosy winter room. The lay-out of these areas emphasises a very traditional set of family roles in that it is easy to imagine the woman cooking, the father at his desk, complete with parallel rule and Anglepoise, and the children playing in the sunken area of the room beneath their gaze.

Tombazis House, Patras, Greece. The master
bedroom follows the well-established 'healthy
simplicity' typology of the modern weekend house
with its use of warm-toned Scandinavian wood
and elegant and unfussy built-in fittings that give
an almost functional aesthetic to what would by
contemporary Greek standards be the luxury of
an en-suite bathroom. The 1970s was a unique
period in architecture, as children's ideas of fun
formed a focus of design as much as parents'
ideas of peace and safety. Here their rooms
continue the healthy aesthetic but with a nautical
inflection in the use of bunks and ladders and
built-in fittings. There are three bunk-beds in each
room. In the 1970s these were seen to be the
acme of a child's room equipment (by children
particularly) despite their impracticality in every
respect except saving space. In these child-
centred rooms, by far the 'coolest' feature would
be the Perspex porthole above the third bunk.

De Vido House

Alfredo De Vido

East Hampton, Long Island, New York, USA   1968-97

The setting for the De Vido House is among the pine barrens, equidistant from East Hampton to the south-east and Sag Harbor to the north-west, and near the sea at Northwest Harbor and Three Mile Harbor. Though the almost urban plenitude of the Hamptons towns is no more than a few miles away, the dense woodland setting and its rich wildlife make the house seem secluded though in fact it is close to a good road. Whereas many Long Island houses seem to depend for their effect on long views the De Vido House is set within its own peaceful introspective world. A great deal of the quality of the house is dependent on its garden, designed with Catherine De Vido, which has been formed with regard to the surrounding trees. The effect of the maintenance of much of the original woodland setting is that the sense of being in an artificial garden appears and disappears at almost every turn. The man-made aspect colludes in these effects, in that it is a low-lying, naturalistic composition that is planted with grasses and low shrubs punctuated by a few specimen trees. The major features of the garden are its shallow pond and its swimming pool, which almost surround the house and seamlessly cross the boundary between a typical, shallow woodland pond, overlooked by a studio, and a formal water feature that wouldn't seem out of place in an Italian Renaissance garden. The swimming pool, which terminates in a formal and rather Japanese pavilion, seems as much a pond as a pool. This subtle combination of the natural and the formal, the uncontrolled and the highly abstract is repeated in the architecture of the house.

Although first planned in the late 1960s and only finished recently, the house was predominantly built in the 1970s. Its form is an unusual and successful synthesis of vernacular and modern forms. The original house, which was formed from a square flanked by lean-to extensions, was later extended by two very similar but half-sized repeats of the main form added onto one side of the original structure. The building as it now appears is an almost Japanese complex of wooden pavilions arranged within a landscape of water and trees, linked either by paths or by being placed side by side. De Vido has spoken of being influenced by three traditions: the American vernacular; Scandinavian design, through time spent in Denmark as a young architect; and traditional Japanese architecture, from his time there as a Seabee with the US Navy. All these influences are evident in this complex, yet with a degree of synthesis that makes each strand apparent but hard to identify specifically. Given De Vido's continuing interest in Japan, it is possible that the building is influenced by similar ideas that affected individual Japanese houses of the 1970s, such as Kisaburo Kawakami's Fu Residence of 1972.

De Vido House, Long Island, USA. The large structure to the left was the first part of the house built in the early 1970s, followed by the smaller structure of similar form to the right, with the porch on the extreme left and the dining extension between the two main sections last. Despite the piecemeal nature of the additions, a repetition of the forms used in the initial structure maintains the unity of the whole, as does the use of grey timber and a hierarchy of sidings, shingles and grills.

De Vido House, Long Island, USA. The exterior language of Scandinavian and Japanese references is supplanted inside by references to American farms and frontier buildings. In many areas the house shows a drift towards an interest in articulating its 'language', making it more complex and symbolic. This is done through the contrast of narrow passages with large rooms, the Mannerist use of rough unplaned cedar planking laid horizontally, and the elaborate staircase, which has two runs that meet on one half-landing and then continues as a single stair to the gallery on the first floor.

Seen from outside, the woodland setting and extensive use of wood and glass recall Scandinavian Modernism, and the complex of similar buildings in a hierarchy placed within a formalisation of nature is Japanese. However, at the core is the spirit of the local wooden vernacular. The local references are not to the salt-box homes of the early settlers, but to the later and larger agricultural buildings – their great, sheltering, airy volumes inspiring the main space of the house.

The original building is made up of two rectangular forms set at right angles. Combined they form a squat cross within a square and above this two-storey structure is a clerestory that rises one more storey. The structure of the building uses the constructional methods used in local barns to create a large open internal space that resembles the aisles and nave of a church. While the lower area is made up of post-and-beam construction, the clerestory level is supported by four beams that cross the centre of the end walls of the clerestory to form a spectacular X form that supports the flat roof above. The 'nave' of this building rises through three floors and is open to the 'aisles' on much of the ground floor, and this unity of space is emphasised by the black quarry tiles that are used throughout the ground floor. This unified area, which forms the main living space of the house, is warmed by a large freestanding stone fireplace in the centre of one of the 'aisles'. Its stone chimney rises up through the gallery of the floor above, which overlooks the central nave.

To either side of the chimney are access passages to the extension that houses the kitchen. Before you reach this, the way is interrupted by a complex stair structure that takes you up behind the chimney onto a wide landing lined with books, and then a gallery that runs around the edge of the nave and from which open two small bedrooms, both with double aspect, and one bathroom. At each end of the gallery on the long sides rise two narrow ladders leading to small study rooms at the clerestory level, both of which run the width of the short sides of the nave and overlook it. Most of the interior space of the main structure overlooks the three-storey-high central nave and this creates a palatial sense of space in what is a small building.

Beyond the firestack and stairs lie the kitchen and dining room. The kitchen has built-in units faced in warm-toned timber to match the interior of

Left and below: **De Vido House, Long Island, USA.** The rustic elements of the house are good examples of the breakdown in the 1970s of the logical and simple internal planning of Modernism in favour of a design practice that is more interested in how spaces are experienced, summed up in Robert Venturi's phrase 'complexity and contradiction'.

the rest of the house, three-quarter-height windows and a skylight. Like most of the rooms and spaces, the dining room has full-height windows and access to the garden. It too has a skylight. Situated beyond this are two master bedrooms with en-suite bathrooms. The bedrooms are like small versions of the principal living area and rise to a double-height space created by a clerestory level in the centre of the cruciform rooms. They are filled with light due to the full-height glazing of the walls on one aspect combined with skylights over the bed space and clerestory lights. The bathrooms have skylights.

Whereas the exterior is clad in horizontal cedar siding and shingles stained and weathered grey, the inside is a mixture of warm-toned, reddish cedar planking interspersed with dark-stained beams and trusses, which gives a Scandinavian feeling. This hierarchical rhythm is further punctuated by a smaller horizontal motif of wooden jalousies that cover many of the internal and external windows, and internal shutters that subtly control both the levels of light and the sense of privacy within the building. One of the most expressive elements of the interior is the use of barely sanded, rough-sawn cedar planking for the walls and door facings, which together with the crudely geometric firestack give the interior an aura of frontier pragmatism.

The total interior effect of the house is of a homage to the American wooden building tradition. This feeling is increased by the attachment to the walls of pieces of early American joinery collected by Al De Vido. These include a sash window, with shutters set in a pediment, that is used to help light the gallery and which came from an old house in New Orleans. To this must be added the constant and surprising internal and external vistas

Opposite: **De Vido House, Long Island, USA.** The interior structure of the house is based on that of barn construction, and this agricultural functionalism is continued in the use of open stairs to access the upper rooms of the house. The inclusion of large architectural antiques shows the emerging interest in pre-industrial Americana in the 1970s, which was epitomised by the fashion for Shaker design later in the decade. Despite the Historicism and the presence of an atrium in all but name, the interior is still open-planned and the fireplace remains modern.

afforded by the circulation spaces in the house, and the varied and diverse light effects that its many windows provide. The complexity of the light, space and cultural references of the De Vido House take it out of the architecture of the Modernist tradition, yet there are none of the shallow surface effects of 'decorated shed' Post-Modernism, and the house is thus firmly placed in the 1970s. The complexity and sophistication of the building is, in no small part, due to Al De Vido's practice as both a speculative housing developer and a primarily domestic architect specialising in upper-middle-income homes. More than the other architects featured in this section, he both had, and has, a professional interest in concepts of home and an equally broad experience of clients' conceptions from which to develop his own multicultural approach.

De Vido House, Long Island, USA. The kitchen and dining room are conventionally Modernist in their fittings, furnishings and the simplicity and rectilinearity of their design. Equally Modern is the use of functional window units and the general concern to increase light levels through maximum fenestration.

Great Western Plantation

Alan Tye
Tring, Buckinghamshire, UK 1975

Tring is a typical small town in the Home Counties, set in rolling chalk hills about 30 miles north of London. It has a large flint and brick church and a fine Queen Anne Revival hotel set on a high street of small, long-established shops, banks and an old country police station. It is now also a wealthy dormitory town for those employed in the capital who are prepared to trade a long daily commute for a home in the country. In the 19th century the town was also home to a branch of the Rothschild family, who lived at Tring Park and established an important natural history museum there. Great West Plantation was originally part of the Rothschild estate that lies on the outskirts of the town and is, as the name suggests, an area of now mature, deciduous trees set on a gentle slope. It was here in 1975 that Alan Tye decided to design and build a home for his family, and a studio for his successful product-design practice.

Although on a very grand site, more arboretum than plantation, the house and studio were designed as a low-cost building that could be built for the same price as a three-bedroom local authority house of the day. Its form and structure are therefore a very simple T-shape. The upright of the T houses the single-storey accommodation wing, while the crossing of the T is made up of a single-storey studio room and a two-storey kitchen and living area. These are separated by a hall at the point where the three areas forming the upright and the crossing of the T meet.

The house–studio is built on a falling site and this was used by the architect to create a double-height space at the end of the house where the living and kitchen area are sited. This is based on Le Corbusier's Pavilion de l'Esprit Nouveau (1925) where a double-height space lit by a double-height, full-width window is divided by a mezzanine. In Tye's design the kitchen and dining area occupy the mezzanine while the 'living room' is on the lower floor.

The exterior of the house is a very simple combination of white-rendered concrete block walls beneath an overhanging flat roof supported by exposed brown–black-stained tree trunks. The walls are punctuated by dark-stained window frames and the unusual device, similar to that used by Le Corbusier in his Maisons Jaoul (1956), of shutters that do not cover the window but instead cover ventilation apertures controlled by an opening door on the inside. This allows the windows to be fixed, non-opening units. This extreme simplicity of the facades creates a starkly simple effect that has been described as a combination of Scandinavian and oriental styles. Most of the windows of the building are small, except for those of the studio where one

Top right: **Great Western Plantation, Tring, UK.** From different positions around the exterior, the house takes on different characteristics. From the living-room elevation *(top right)* the main feature is the Corbusian double-height window lightly framed by the white wall and a black roofline. The large windows that make up the glass wall are slightly set back, which reduces reflection and makes the glazed area appear dark. This helps to create an overall effect of monumentality, which is absent from the other elevations, from this aspect.

Above and right: **Great Western Plantation, Tring, UK.** The combination of a small-scale garden, the complex mix of planes created by the court of buildings around the entrance, and the rustic simplicity of their construction evokes a feeling of oriental design at the approach to the house. By contrast, the kitchen exterior, which shares a small garden and veranda with the family wing of the house, looks more like a Scandinavian holiday home. This mixture of elements is an accurate reflection of the influences on the architect, in part cultural, in part generational, and they are also reflected in the interiors of the house.

Opposite: **Great Western Plantation, Tring, UK.** Throughout the house the wall and roof treatments are the same, and the floors – tiled in areas subjected to heavy wear or dampness, wood in the family wing and carpeted in the living area – are all in shades of beige. The stairs and radiator surfaces are steel, patinated dark brown, and act as a counterpoint to the white walls and pale flooring. The device of using thin metal plates for stair treads, which are set into an incline covered in the tiling used on the floor, was used by the architect to create a sense that the spaces within the house are continuous despite being on different levels. This sense of continuous space is also emphasised by gestures like the long corridor shelf that forms an extension of the hall floor, which incidentally increases the sense of scale of the hall area where it leads to the family rooms.

Above: **Great Western Plantation, Tring, UK.** The windows have a similar ventilation system to that used by Le Corbusier in his Maisons Jaoul and this allows the windows to be fixed units. Throughout the house dark-wood Venetian blinds are used instead of curtains. This allows subtle controls of light levels and effects that emphasise the serenity of the interior.

facade is entirely glazed from floor to ceiling, the living–kitchen area where the double-height facade is completely glazed in six panels, and the master bedroom which has a wide picture window.

The severe simplicity of the facades acts as a foil for the beautiful Modernist garden designed by Peter Aldington OBE, which expertly mixes very low planting and specimen trees and shrubs to create a rather formal landscape at the front of the building. The view from the studio is of a much wilder, more natural, but enclosed composition of grasses and small trees, while the view from the children's rooms and the kitchen–living area is across a sweeping lawn beneath the mature beech and oak trees of the plantation. The view from the master bedroom is the most surprising in that here Aldington has created a very restricted and intimate view of grasses and hedgerow plants, shrubs and trees that seem to crowd in around the window.

In front of the main entrance to the house, there is a separate entry for the studio and a flat-roofed, open porch on a plinth reached by a short run of full-width stairs. The stairs and the plinth are tiled in beige. The wide front door is made of teak planking. The door furniture is the architect's own Modric design. Inside, the beige tiling continues throughout the hall, which has three exits. Throughout the building the walls are painted white. To the left a short passage runs past a small guest room, by the front door, to a flight of stairs leading up to the studio. The stairs throughout the house all have the same unique structure. The tiled floor does not end at the stairs but instead continues up an incline to the level of the floor above. Into this incline are fitted deep steel treads about half an inch thick finished in an oxidised patina that has become polished over the years. Incidentally, the same finish is used for the radiator covers throughout the house. The studio is a simple, large rectangular space with full-height and -width fenestration on one side that opens onto a patio and overlooks its own secluded garden area. The garden is defined by the rising land on one side, the walls of the bedroom wing of the house on the other and a hedgerow at the end.

Opposite the front door, across the hall and down a short flight of stairs, lies the bedroom wing of the house. The bedrooms are arranged in a row down the wing and are accessed by a corridor lit by a window at the hall end and skylights down its length. At the hall end is a large bathroom for guests and the children, which has Tye-designed handbasins set at adult and child height, all fitted with the designer's own Admix taps . Beyond this lie the three children's rooms. As in the rest of the house, the door apertures run the full height of the walls and the gap above the door is filled in with a panel. The doors themselves are of the flush-panel type, fitted with stainless-steel hinges and stainless-steel Modric door furniture. Inside the bedrooms there are child-sized built-in cupboards finished in white, built-in single beds and, under the wide windows, built-in beech desktops which give the rooms a

Left and previous page: Great Western Plantation, Tring, UK. The interior of the living area is very much as it was when it was first built, as is evidenced by the Bang and Olufsen quadrophonic stereo equipment and the Swiss modular, flexible, sofa in light and dark brown leather. The kitchen combines the European U-shaped galley design with American scale and features, such as the breakfast bar and the treatment of the dining area, which is more diner than dining room.

Right: Great Western Plantation, Tring, UK. The kitchen and living area, very much in the spirit of Le Corbusier's Pavilion de l'Esprit Nouveau, provides an integrated and spacious living centre, easily sufficient for the family of five that the house was designed for. The monochromatic colour scheme, which in a typically 1970s manner substitutes shades of brown for the black of the earlier 1960s architects' houses, creates a sense of contemporary, minimalist, almost Zen-like, calm. This is intentional as the Tye design practice has an approach that applies Eastern philosophies to its design problems, with the aim of creating 'healthy' industrial design.

rather academic feeling, though conforming to the child-friendly design ideas of the day.

At the end of the corridor is a brown-tiled master bathroom fitted with the designer's Meridian bathroom fittings and his Admix taps. Beyond this the master bedroom is very simply laid out with fitted cupboards and a bed that faces the garden through a picture window.

Immediately to the right of the front door are stairs down to the living area. Next to the opening for the stairs, a tiled landing runs past a utility room and continues into the mezzanine kitchen–dining area. The mezzanine, edged by a low parapet, looks out over the stairwell and the living room to where there is a huge double-height and full-width window. It also has its own picture windows overlooking the garden and a veranda. The kitchen is at the back of the mezzanine and is separated from the dining area by a large run of custom-built beech units separated into two blocks: a bench unit and, at eye level, another set of storage units. This is mirrored on the back wall of the room. The units that divide the kitchen from the dining area feature a breakfast-bar – with a black, padded recess into which legs can be fitted – and a series of beech panels that can be pulled down from the units above to fully separate the kitchen from the dining area. Into the stainless-steel worktop of the bench are set four Creda electric cooking rings, while into the unit above them is fitted an extractor. The kitchen is lit by a glass door, which opens onto a veranda. This runs around the outside of the kitchen and the utility room, and continues along the length of the bedroom wing.

Steel-plate stairs down from the hall lead to the living room, which is partly single-height below the mezzanine and partly a vast double-height space lit by the huge six-panel window. As in the rest of the house, the light here is controlled by wooden Venetian blinds worked by electric motors. The floor is covered by a dark beige, woollen fitted carpet. On the back wall, below the mezzanine and running its length, is a beige-tiled plinth and on top of this is a recessed, wood-burning fireplace surrounded by dark-brown flush panels, behind which are cabinets and access to the utility room. Overlooking the fire is an enormous Swiss-designed sofa made up of flexible, light and dark brown, leather-upholstered sections arranged as an open circle.

INDEPENDENT

It is a temptation in any account of architecture to avoid the exception, the tangential or the unusual in order to present a coherent, controlled and encapsulating position. Such an exercise is particularly inappropriate in any account of the architecture of the 1970s since the rebellious intellectual spirit of 1968 found its concrete individualistic expression in the decade that followed, either in the form of optimistic explorations of the 'liberations' of the 1960s or later in the nihilistic rejections of Punk and its political equivalent, Neo-Conservatism. Leaving aside any ethical considerations, the 1970s was also when the nascent fashion and music consumerism of the 1960s extended until the application of the values of the boutique to our day-to-day existence became summed up in the term 'lifestyle'. The critical intellectual revolution of the 1960s also expressed a longer lasting trend towards a lack of deference, and although this is often presented as a negative it actually indicated a new independence of spirit throughout society. Equally, the rampant growth of consumerism can be regarded as a product of this increasing independence, which in this context is more usually termed 'individualism'.

Independent

Any account of the *'casa unifamiliare'* architecture of the 1970s should include some houses that represent these values. Although they do not give any sense of an emerging architectural movement, they do offer a view of the effects of the growth of consumerism and individualism on architects and their clients, who should now be retermed 'consumers' to reflect the new, more complicated, relationship between them. The 1970s was also a period when independence of mind was less than usually out of step with the spirit of the age, which preferred heterogeneity to homogeneity and accommodated aesthetic difference more easily than we do now, despite our firm belief to the opposite.

Paradoxically, independent, in the sense of not depending on authority or indeed anything for validation, is the term that offers the best sense of collective similarity for the houses in this section since there are few other points of contact between these very different buildings. One thing that does unify them is the symbiotic independence of architect and client, the desire of one giving the space to create form in the other.

The Manser House in Blackheath, London, is the product of a very long client–architect relationship between Patrick Gwynne and the speculative developer Leslie Bilsby. They first met in the 1930s when Gwynne had used Bilsby as a consultant for the built-in cabinets in his parent's house, The Homewood at Esher, Surrey (1937), now owned by the National Trust. In 1949, in turn, Bilsby commissioned Gwynne to reconstruct a bombed Victorian house at 115 Blackheath Park and afterwards continued to commission a number of houses from him, although most of these were never built. One such project, dating from 1960, was a house made of three circular pavilions, although, as Gwynne noted on the project archive, 'the site was abandoned because the site was not really sufficiently attractive for the design which materialised'. The design resembled his later one for Park Gate.

By 1960 Bilsby was the developer for the conventionally Modernist SPAN houses designed by Eric Lyons. The contrast between Gwynne and Lyons could not be greater or more indicative of Gwynne's total independence from the architectural mainstream as represented by Lyons' work for Bilsby. Perhaps because of Bilsby's speculative work he wanted something very individual for himself and he certainly got this in his next house from Gwynne, built in 1969 at 10 Blackheath Park – a three-storey, double-fronted house faced with slate and smoked glass, accessed from a circular stair and a drawbridge the design of which was based on a recurring pentangular module. After his wife died Bilsby commissioned another house from Gwynne in 1978 at Park Gate, also in Blackheath, which is featured here. This was designed to suit his resurgent single status and featured only two bedrooms. It was a kind of folly on his return to bachelor status. In retrospect, Bilsby was a very modern consumer, although unusual in that he consumed architecture in the way that other rich men buy cars or yachts. Gwynne, though often represented as an oddball architect out of step with new developments, was in retrospect much more in touch with changing contemporary taste than he was usually given credit for, since he understood the principles of styling. Where his 1960 pavilion building has a Buckminster Fulleresque techno-centric styling his 1979 version is re-presented as an idiosyncratic masculine Brutalism that reflected his client's desires. Between them Gwynne and Bilsby left the mainstream of British architectural taste a long way behind in their creation of architecture that is only now becoming generally admired.

The other close client–architect relationship represented here is that between Al De Vido and Leonard McCombe. The American architectural context is different to that in many other countries because of the relatively cheap costs of building and land and the relative affluence of the population. This has created a much bigger market for individually designed homes going right back to the late 1940s, and there is a much more developed consumer market for architecture in America. Although there is a lot of individualism in American architect-designed houses, this is really the individualism of product diffusion – everything is individual but the same. This is what the developed consumer expects. Individuality is recognised by a niche product produced from a recognisably high-quality branded range, just as with a Mercedes car. On Long Island the standard branded architecture of the 1970s was a variation on the theme of the New York Five. Though Al De Vido has also built in this style (see his Sametz House, p 86) he has never really worked in a style but has varied the aesthetic of his designs to meet the needs of a combination of other conditions that also determine architecture.

At the McCombe House the client set the pace for design as much as any other factor. When his house was built, Leonard McCombe was a photographer for *Time* magazine and before that had been a war photographer. Originally from the Isle of Man, he is fiercely private and with his wife, another European immigrant, and sons he bought a large well-wooded fruit farm in a remote part of Long Island as a retreat, far from the fashionable Hamptons.

Theatre Royal, York, UK. The complex of tent-like forms enclosed by a glass wall is the most likely source for the form of Gwynne's pavilions at Park Gate as well as an earlier circular group designed for Bilsby but never built. Both show that the Manser House had a very long gestation of nearly 20 years. Though the surface treatments adapted to the architectural fashions of the day, through the Brutalism of Park Gate may have been dated by 1979, Gwynne was fundamentally an individualist who stood slightly aside from the mainstream throughout a very long career that spanned almost the entire period of Modernism.

The site for the house that he commissioned De Vido to build is as far from the intrusions of the outside world as possible. The house itself is unique among De Vido's *oeuvre* in the materials used. Whereas, in common with the practice of most Long Island architects, most of his work is finished in wood this building is faced with large stones. This is because the client, McCombe, specified that he wanted his house covered in stones that he had personally picked off the beach below his property. However, with the exception of the chimneys, the building is not made of stone but has a locally conventional wooden frame. McCombe and his sons also took part in the construction of the house and have since modified the design. What one senses at the McCombe House is that the client engaged the architect to realise his vision of a house, rather than engaging him to have the vision and design it, as was the practice with an architect like Jaffe. In this respect the McCombe House represents a newly emergent trend in modern architecture where the client has a more directive role and can determine not only the number of bathrooms but also the aesthetic of the design. Equally, De Vido is a new kind of architect who is confident enough in his own position to enter what is in effect a collaboration between architect and client.

The same cannot be said of the practice of Gian Piero Frassinelli, who works in the old tradition of the form giver. At the same time he has a very complex attitude to his work, which has been strongly affected by the countercultural atmosphere of his student years at Florence in the 1960s. After graduating from the architecture school in Florence in 1968, though at the time it was occupied by students, Frassinelli went on to join the Superstudio group at the end of the same year. Thus, he was in a radical theoretical architecture group before he began to practise, and here the primary activity was a critique of current architectural practice to the extent that the group proposed an end to architecture. In 1972 he built the remarkable triangular Villa Taddei. Although there are other triangular buildings of the period in Italy, like Zanusso's house on Lake Como, and examples elsewhere, like Noyes' 1974 Johnson House near Mystic in Connecticut, the architects use conventional aesthetic approaches to create aesthetic and beautiful interiors, and the buildings are in fantastic positions by a lake or on an island. Frassinelli's house is so idiosyncratic that it seems to be hostile to its site, which it fills almost completely. Its context is a conventional suburb, and its inhabitants find almost all the interior made subordinate to a great roof over a large living area with one huge window with no view. In fact the house is easier to read as a physical critique of its surroundings than as a conventionally desirable home. The architect has said of his own practice that he has not found architecture but that he also knows what he did not want to find:

'First of all let us see what I did NOT want to find:
I did NOT want to find a monumental architecture.
I did NOT want to find a fashionable architecture.
I did NOT want to find a beautiful architecture.

Instead I always sought a 'skinless' architecture, an architecture in which the outside arises from the inside, straight out of the inner life of the men who live it.'[1]

Haus Böttcher, Berlin, Germany. Haus Böttcher epitomises the new independence in domestic architecture that emerged during the 1970s. The entire house and most of its contents were either designed or made by its owner, Wolfgang Böttcher.

This fundamentally oppositional stance is well represented in the Villa Taddei though moderated by Frassinelli's affection for local vernacular and craft traditions, and this is the essence of his independence – he stands as a critic of architecture and a lover of quotidian building. There is nothing remarkable in a young architect of the 1970s adopting this position for the worker and against The Man, but what is surprising is that Frassinelli actually incorporates his politics into his buildings.

In its own quiet way Haus Bottcher in the Berlin suburb of Rudow is as representative of the oppositional politics of the 1960s and 1970s as anything by Superstudio, as it embodies the discourses of self-reliance that were mobilised by the Green movement and the counterculture generally to give people a means of operating outside Culture with a capital C. Haus Bottcher represents the kind of independence of action that informed the self-build movement that grew up in Europe and America during the 1970s. The self-build was based on the easy availability of mass-produced, semi-prefabricated components and system building ranges that proliferated in the 1960s to meet the demands for quick construction where there were labour shortages. In the 1970s both architects and other groups, such as communes and housing associations, realised that building products that could be bought off the shelf offered the unskilled the possibility of designing and building their own home providing this was done within ranges of standard parts. Often it was architects who led such schemes, as in the case of Walter Segal, a German refugee who settled in London. In the 1970s, after a career working on small projects, he designed a self-build house, found funding within the London local authorities and managed the construction of a small estate of self-built houses in south London, first at Segal Close, Lewisham, in 1977 and then Walters Way, Brockley, finished in 1982. Another example of the self-build principle is the Hopkins House in Hampstead, finished in 1976, which was built from components available in the construction industry for use in factory or warehouse units by relatively unskilled labour, with specialist subcontractors, where necessary, managed by the owner.

Haus Böttcher lies somewhere between these two examples and in some ways extends beyond them. Wolfgang Böttcher was by training a blacksmith and by profession a steel merchant, so when he decided to build his own house he knew what to build it from and how to put it together. However, he had the sense to let someone else design it and employed the architects Wolfgang Goschel and Rosemarie Barthel to produce a plan, although it was Böttcher himself who designed the steel joints of the house frames. Once he had the plans he set to work building the house himself in its entirety, as well as designing and making most of the furniture. Begun in 1976 and finished in 1979, it has the some of the High-Tech finesse of the Hopkins House, and certainly the same standard of construction, but the intangible satisfaction of the house belongs to the family that built it, particularly Böttcher himself since it is peculiarly his own creation, a statement of self and of complete independence.

1   Peter Lang and William Menking, *Superstudio: A Life Without Objects*, Skira Editore (Milan), 2003, pp 82–3.

Villa Taddei

Gian Piero Frassinelli
Santa Croce sull'Arno, Pisa, Italy   1972

Santa Croce sull'Arno lies almost equidistant between Pisa and Florence on the Pisa side of the flat Arno valley. It is a semi-industrialised town specialising in leather processing and manufacturing. At its edge, on a corner plot on the periphery of a suburban district adjacent to a light industrial estate, lies the Villa Taddei, an extraordinary piece of architecture parachuted into a very ordinary residential street. Behind an equally conventional well-clipped hedge the house presents its extraordinary profile of common red brick.

The form of Villa Taddei is as if a pyramid made of four equilateral triangles has been bisected and laid on the ground on the side of the bisection. At its apex it rises through three floors while an equilateral triangle forms the roof, which slopes down to a retaining wall hidden by a turfed glacis that continues the form of the roof down to the ground level. Into this Toblerone-on-its-side structure are cut several openings. Where the roof meets the retaining wall on the roof facade is a 7 or 8-metre-long opening, 2.5 metres high, that forms the window for the living area. On the two vertical faces are cut five openings. On one side a ramp leads down to a basement garage. Next to this is a square void to a recessed double door, and moving along 4 metres or so another 4-metre void is made up of two full-height glazed bays 1 metre wide. These are separated by a recessed balcony about 2 metres square that begins on the first floor and is open to the roof. On the adjacent vertical facade there are only two voids, one above the other. The lower one is 2 metres wide with an angled double door, one edge to the outside wall the other set back 1 metre, while the upper one, which forms an internal balcony, is 2 metres square and open to the roof. The exterior glazing is made up of various adaptations of a basic grid of glazed squares set in a heavy, varnished iroko frame. On the living area side, where the roof extends to the ground, the building is turfed with grass, to a height equal to that of the living area windows. Above this the roof is tiled in a modern version of Roman tiles. Over the living area windows is a striped awning.

The house can be entered from four places. Double doors give access from the two vertical facades, there is an entrance from the garage that comes into the kitchen and the garden can be accessed from the living area windows, which include two sets of French windows at either end. The principal entrance is from the facade with the garage ramp, and this gives onto a short corridor, with cloakroom, that opens into a hall that opens into a kitchen to the left and the main living area to the right. The living space is divided into two parts: a large ground-floor area with an exit leading from the end opposite the kitchen and, continuing round to the right, an L-flight of stairs up to a mezzanine. Continuing back towards the kitchen at the far end

Above and top right: Villa Taddei, Pisa, Italy. The side entrance door is set at an angle that corresponds to the angle at which the internal hallway enters the living area, while on the roof facade the triangular form of the roof is continued to the ground by turf infills to the outside wall, the position of which is marked by the recessed windows of the living area that are the only openings on this facade.

Right: Villa Taddei, Pisa, Italy. The Villa Taddei faces onto a modern suburban street of mainly detached houses. At the extreme left is the front door and below it, further to the left, the ramp to an underground garage. The glazed bay that runs the full height of the building houses a study on the ground floor and the principal bedrooms above. The windows to the bedrooms sit on either side of, but do not overlook, an internal balcony on the first floor accessed from the mezzanine. The gold frames on some of the windows are the anodised aluminium frames of mosquito screens. On the other vertical facade is a similar but smaller balcony with windows for the main bedroom. The brickwork, the rhythm of the large glazed void and the grid created by the window frames on the street facade recall the old ventilated brick barns of the low-lying countryside of the Arno valley.

Villa Taddei, Pisa, Italy. The vast, two-level, quarry-tiled living area of the villa lies beneath an even vaster rural ceiling in a design that gives the sense that the bedrooms and the mezzanine are almost separate buildings contained within one large hall. The long, low garden windows of the ground floor are balanced by the two tall and narrow balcony windows that light the mezzanine and the roof area of the lower space. This creates an effect that seems to make the interior space look bigger. As with other Frassinelli buildings, the windows are mainly for light and air, like an apartment in a crowded city, as none of them offer what would usually be considered a view.

of the living area there is the hall. Facing the garden on the back wall of the hall are double, unglazed but gridded, doors to a study–dining room. The principal feature of the interior is the vast living area on two levels nestling under a traditional farmhouse roof of longitudinal rafters supported by two huge horizontal beams, the spaces between which are plastered. The floors are made up of rectangular glazed floor tiles in a brown that matches the chestnut colour of the varnished woodwork of the ceiling and windows.

Upstairs the mezzanine overlooks the living area from a solid balustrade and, looking the other way, gives onto the two balconies through double doors in an iroko-framed grid that rises the full height of the building. On both sides of the bays there are bedrooms and two bathrooms. The bedrooms are next to the bays but do not have windows looking onto them; rather, they look out through full-height windows in the wooden frame used throughout the house. The external sides of the bays are made from narrow vertical siding. At the apex of the house looking out from the principal bay on the garage facade is a further bedroom accessed by a staircase leading up from the mezzanine and inside this space is a further mezzanine, accessed by a spiral stair.

The Villa Taddei shares with Frassinelli's other work an almost agoraphobic interiority that relates to his stated desire to create an architecture that works from the inside out. Similarities to individual elements of other works are also found synthesised together here. The assertive form of the exterior appears almost as a reaction to the conventionality of its surroundings, as his Piazza San Giovanni apartment in Florence reacts against its Renaissance view. The Villa Taddei also seems to relate to the gnomic comment at the end of his brief remarks on his Superstudio architecture in Lang and Menking's *Superstudio: A Life Without Objects* where he quotes Bernard Tschumi almost as a cipher to his work: 'An architecture can be consciously negative, it can be intentionally designed to be unpleasant, uncomfortable, not to work.' However, such comments should be measured against the villa's continual occupation and its recent acquisition by a new owner, which suggest that the house has none of these characteristics. At a more formal level the villa combines the interest in the crafts evident in the lovingly cleaned and exposed roof of Frassinelli's Casa Fabi at Como and the delight in local vernacular architecture seen in his sensitive modernisation of the Casale Fontibucci near Florence. In the case of the Villa Taddei the vernacular references are to the fantastic ventilated barns of the area between Florence, Pisa and Lucca, with their brick construction interspersed by facades of tiles turned at 45 degrees to the wall to catch the rare breezes in the humid valleys.

McCombe House

Alfredo De Vido

Riverhead, Long Island, New York, USA   1973

Leonard McCombe met Al De Vido when McCombe, a photographer for *Time* magazine, was photographing a house De Vido had designed, and in 1973 he commissioned a new farmhouse from the architect for his farm at the beginning of the North Fork of Long Island. The North Fork differs from the more populous southern side of Long Island in that it retains its original rural character of fruit and arable farms, and the landscape rises to an escarpment where it meets the sea. The old 19th-century clapboard McCombe farmhouse stands on the highway at the junction between the road to the east end of the North Fork and the road running south through Riverhead to the Hamptons. It occupies a large estate of isolated land between the highway and the coast overlooking Long Island Sound.

The new McCombe house is set among the mature deciduous woods that protect the 100 acres of fruit orchards from the hard winters that can affect Long Island's usually benign climate. It lies at the end of a long, wooded drive on the edge of a bluff high above the sea, surrounded by woods that shelter deer and the famous Red Cardinal among trees that stand taller than the three storeys of the house. The only property nearby is an old Art Deco villa built in the 1930s for a Madison Avenue advertising agent and recently converted to a family home by one of Leonard McCombe's sons.

To call De Vido's design for the McCombe House a farmhouse is a misnomer, since it has much more in common with the rugged patrician grandeur of a late 19th-century shooting lodge than with the old farmhouse at the entrance to the McCombe land. Standing on a plinth on its bluff high above the ocean, the house is made up of a number of blocks rising through one and two storeys surrounding a central block of three storeys. This agglomeration of cubic additions, the site and the articulation of the surface in a varying rhythm of horizontal cypress boards and large black-framed windows set against a backdrop of large fieldstones that were taken from the beach below all combine to give the building a martial appearance that goes well with its self-conscious isolation.

Above: **McCombe House, Long Island, USA.** The house stands on its own, on a high bluff overlooking Long Island Sound. The growth under the mature deciduous trees is regularly cut back so that the views can be enjoyed at all times.

Right: **McCombe House, Long Island, USA.** The house, though mostly timber framed, is clad in fieldstones collected from the beach below, giving it a rather grand, martial appearance more common in the late 19th-century retreats further down the coast towards New York. The entrance facade features a gallery or greenhouse separated from the house by a covered drive that forms a *porte-cochere*. On the facades that overlook the ground running towards the sea are glass-box living rooms with balconied bedrooms above them. These surround the central three-storey block of the hall and top-floor bedrooms and studio, and this agglomeration of cuboid forms culminating in the keep-like centre block adds to the 'historic' presence of the house from a distance

The house is a mixed metaphor of Edwardian spaces and 20th-century affluence, which is suggested even as one arrives by the *porte-cochere* effect created at the front of the house by the large Miesian greenhouse that is separated from the main body by a covered drive-through entrance. On entering, one is again struck by the seamless combination of the old-fashioned and the new – directly by the front door is a large comforting stove and, looking up, one sees a large, very high space overlooked by a cantilevered balcony, while across the room populated by comfy upholstered and cushioned chairs is a grand piano set on a slate floor against a wall of massive, carefully harmonised fieldstones. Looking up again, the balcony and the upper walls are all clad in vertical American oak sidings with white ceilings throughout.

The use of different designs that reflect different conceptions of affluence does not end in the hall. To the right of the hall, past the stairs to the lower and upper parts of the house, is the door to the vast kitchen–dining area divided into two spaces that resemble a very upmarket diner. At one end of the room is a large well-appointed fitted kitchen tiled in rectangular, orange flambé tiles while at the other an upholstered bench runs along the wall in

McCombe House, Long Island, USA. While clearly Modern the interior spaces, their relationship to each other and their furnishing recall the country retreats of the late 19th century. The large entrance hall with its balcony, stone walls, grand piano and the fire by the entrance contrast with the overstuffed furnishings with the result that a tension that recalls an older style of living is created between formality and relaxation.

McCombe House, Long Island, USA. Though the mainly glass room that overlooks the sea is very modern, its comfortable English-style furnishing is more like that of a drawing room than the Modernist environment that it might be and of which an Eames recliner *(glimpsed in the distance, opposite)* is emblematic. Part of this out-of-time quality is a result of the way that the use and décor of the house subtly undermine the usually dominant Modern architecture, as can be seen in the handling of the transition between the main hall and the sitting room.

front of a large table and looks out through the woods towards the ocean through a full-height picture window. Retreating back into the entrance hall and turning right, there is a large low room that looks out on three sides through a full-height curtain wall. This is joined to the main hall by a short wall lined with book-filled shelves. The remaining inner wall has a central chimney breast of fieldstones with a large wide, wood-burning stove and, to its right as one looks back towards the centre of the house, is a neat range of built-in units that function as a drinks cabinet or sideboard. This glass-box space is furnished like an English drawing room with the exception of an Eames recliner by the window. There is another similar room with a fire on the south side of the main hall that functions as a study, and looks out over a chine towards the other family house a few hundred yards away.

Returning to the stairs and heading down there is an indoor pool and another recreation room. Going upstairs through half-landing turns one comes to the balcony. This passes two children's rooms with their own balconies and leads to the master bedroom, which enjoys a double aspect with the main view towards the ocean through windows that open onto a balcony over the drawing room below. Like the upper levels of the hall, the

Left and opposite: **McCombe House, Long Island, USA.** Another design feature that alters the 'feel' of the building is the use of a complex design rhetoric. In the case of the balcony canti-levered over the main hall there is a reference to the language of the stately home, but this is moderated by the utilitarian rhetoric of the plain oak siding of the walls and the undecorated white ceiling.

Below: **McCombe House, Long Island, USA.** The contrast of affluence and restraint is also apparent in the design of the bedrooms. Though their design includes balconies and their position gives commanding views across the estate, the use of plain oak for the walls and the simple forms of the windows and built-in units give the rooms an ascetic simplicity.

bedrooms are lined with vertical American oak siding and have a restrained simplicity that seems appropriate to the character of the client. Up more stairs there are more bedrooms and a studio for McCombe himself. The bathrooms are simple and fitted with standard American fittings.

Since the house was finished there have been minor alterations that have made it easier to heat. The first of these was the roofing over of the third level of the hall, which really acted only as a skylight. The second was that the original open fires have been replaced by stoves.

The cooperation in design between the owner and the architect has created a house that combines a number of different architectural modes of address which, although all Modernist, come from different interpretations of design for contemporary life, comfort and relationship to the land. The effect of this combination is to create a house that stands apart from the Long Island architectural fashions of the 1960s and 1970s, and has its own paradoxical aura of timeless modernity.

Haus Böttcher

Wolfgang Goschel and Rosemarie Barthel
Gros-Ziethener Chaussee, Rudow, Berlin, Germany   1976-79

Rudow is a quiet, unpretentious suburb at the southern extremity of Berlin. Beyond it lies the rich farmland and ancient walled towns of Brandenburg and beyond to Dresden. The village of Rudow became developed in the early 20th century and there are still many small, cheaply built, brick bungalows along the ribbon-developed roads leading out into the country. Despite its proximity to the massive Gropius Bau housing development, it is not the sort of place that you expect to find a an architect-designed 1970s villa.

The Haus Böttcher lies down a birch-lined suburban street that leads from Rudow's charmless shopping centre. Hidden behind a screen of trees, the house is almost invisible from the road and so its uncompromising modernity and urbanity comes as a bit of a surprise. The exterior is a simple box clad in painted corrugated-steel cladding. The front facade is broken at the centre by a long run of four glazed double doors that open onto the narrow veranda at the front. To the left of centre of this run one pair of doors is extended upwards into a pediment.

Above this is another taller range of long windows and doors, this time arranged in three groups of three with the centre three stepped back and extending up into what used to be called a studio window that extends up to the roof at an angle. These windows and doors also give onto a veranda. The rear elevation is much simpler and is pierced by small window apertures, with the exception of two French windows for the bedrooms on the first floor and a door from Wolfgang Böttcher's study onto the rear veranda. The window and door frames are primary yellow in contrast to the very pale grey cladding – very 1980s, very High-Tech.

The owners of the house, a steel merchant and an accountant, are far from the type of client expected of an architect or designer who might have built such a structure in the 1970s but, though the epitome of Berliner respectability, they are even more remarkable than anyone might imagine. Not only did they employ the architects Wolfgang Goschel and Rosemarie Barthel to design them a house in the garden of a 1920s bungalow belonging to Wolfgang Böttcher's mother but, a blacksmith by training, Böttcher built the entire house himself from the excavation of the site upwards. Nor was this the kind of self-build where prefabrication is prevalent. In the basement is all the heavy equipment required to fabricate the structure of the house, which is constructed using a steel frame and clad in steel. Incidentally, this frame defines the outline of the lozenge-shaped windows as they fit between X frames. Wolfgang Böttcher built everything in the house, even the furniture (easy to say but hard to do), and his partner provided paintings and sculptures

Above: **Haus Böttcher, Berlin, Germany.** Almost the only expressive feature of an otherwise very calm design is the front door, which without the decoration would simply read as a side door.

Opposite: **Haus Böttcher, Berlin, Germany.** The exterior of the house is clad in painted steel panels applied to a steel frame. The house is fundamentally a cube except that it has been cut into on the upper floor to provide a studio window. The frame is cross-braced and this internal structure is expressed in the window apertures of the entrance to the living-dining area from the veranda on the ground floor, and the window to the reading area on the first floor. At the rear, cross-bracing cuts across the front of the upstairs bathroom window. On either side of the bathroom French windows from the bedrooms look out over the garden, but this design is a modification and they were originally intended to lead out onto a balcony that would then lead down to the garden. Many of the architects' original plans were not used in the construction of the house, which is simpler and cleaner in design as a result.

for their home. The published plans of the house differ markedly from what was built in both interior and exterior details and seem to be a rationalisation of some of the details of the architects' plans.

Perhaps the most remarkable thing about the Haus Bottcher is the perfection of its finish. Without exception every detail is beautifully done and even the steel-framed chairs and sofas, which could well have been a disaster of crude good intentions, are completely successful and rather Corbusian in feel.

The house is built on three floors. The basement houses storage and utility spaces, and Wolfgang Böttcher's workshop. This is entered through a large open porch, partly below ground level, created by a roof that also forms the rear veranda for the study area at the back of the house. This overlooks the newly restored old bungalow further down the typical Berlin garden in which grass and fruit trees predominate. There is also an open veranda at the front of the house giving access to the front garden from the dining–living area. The main floor of the house is entered via a short stairway and a steel door at the side of the house. This leads into a small hall with the main living area through a door straight ahead, a stairway with a return to the upper floor and a cloakroom to the right. This area is predominantly white, functional and simple. It is distinguished by the high ceilings, nearly 3 metres, and the equally high doors between areas, though there are few of these as the house is very open. At two points in the large open areas of both floors, which

Above and opposite: **Haus Böttcher, Berlin, Germany.** The whole of the interior, with the exception of the dining chairs, curtains and lamps, was designed and built by the owner. The interior spaces on both floors are very open, with individual rooms sited at the back of the building so that around 65 per cent of the house is given over to two open-planned areas for living. On the ground floor, the space is used as a living, dining and reading area, with a separate area for TV-watching off to one side.

Left: **Haus Bottcher, Berlin, Germany.** The basement contains the equipment and machinery used in the construction of the house, which was built almost entirely by its owner who is a qualified blacksmith.

Haus Böttcher, Berlin, Germany. Upstairs is a large, well-lit studio space, with a library area to one side. As on the ground floor the furniture in the room was designed and built by Wolfgang Böttcher – with the exception of the Jacobsen Ant chairs and the reclaimed sideboard, though this has been personalised by the owners. The bedrooms and bathrooms of the house are small and treated as service areas in the Modernist domestic tradition.

could be mistaken for American 'lofts', two plastered steel girders hold up the floor and roof above them. The floors are tightly laid blonde pine, which is traditional in many Berlin houses.

The living area is formed like an L with the long side to the front of the house. At one side there is an open-planned fitted kitchen in yellow and a dining area that runs into the sitting area at the other end of the facade. On the short side of the L, running back into the house, is the TV watching and reading area. To the rear of the house, overlooking the garden, are two studies divided at the centre by a bathroom.

The upper floor has a large open room facing the front of the house, which is lit by a skylight as well as large windows. This leisure/study area is surrounded by three bedrooms, with French windows and a bathroom that is positioned over that on the ground floor. A mixture of Wolfgang Böttcher's steel-framed sofas and Typenmobel furniture of the early 20th century – which Gertraude Böttcher has painted – occupies the space, creating a sense of a mid-1980s Ron Arad interior. The simplicity of the house, and its scale, create a sense of space and peace but its large social spaces are gained at the expense of the private rooms, which are quite small. The greatest quality of the house is its lightness; a real virtue in a northern city like Berlin.

The combination of utility, practicality and light gives the house a feeling not unlike that of the large, detached, faintly Modernist houses of Britain's more advanced 1950s suburbs; correct, conservative but forward looking – suggestive of solidity and liberality. The Haus Böttcher has all these qualities and despite its assertive use of industrial materials and spaces the interior wears its modernity with discreet good manners.

Manser House

Patrick Gwynne

Park Gate, Blackheath, London, UK   1979

Blackheath is one of London's famous villages, though less so than Highgate or Hampstead, and like them throughout the 20th century it was home to the more artistic and Bohemian kind of Londoner, as well as the more usual civil servants and businessmen. It was also popular with architects, because after the Second World War it was possible to buy and build cheaply on sites set in the mature sylvan hinterland of the Georgian and Victorian gardens of the Cator Estate. From the late 1950s through into the 1980s many award-winning estates of modern family houses were built in the grounds of these old houses by the SPAN company of the architect Eric Lyons and his partner, the developer Leslie Bilsby. By the late 1960s Bilsby was a very rich man and he was able to commission Patrick Gwynne, his friend since the 1930s, to build him a large double-fronted house on the main road of the Cator Estate, Blackheath Park. But in the mid-1970s he became a widower and asked Gwynne to build him a new smaller house in a more secluded part of the estate.

Close to his old house, 10 Blackheath Park, is a footpath that runs between high privet hedges out into an unmade-up road, Park Gate. Passing downhill between houses built in the 1950s and ornamented with recovered Georgian details, and then past large 1930s detached residences, one comes to an early SPAN estate of low-rise terraces of flats around garden courtyards. Next to this, on the same side of the road, Gwynne built Park Gate on a parcel of land fringed by mature trees bordering a brook running the length of its very deep garden. It is a falling site with a 50-foot frontage, and the house is set well back from the road behind a Modernist shrub garden separated from a gravelled drive by a path of reclaimed granite setts.

According to Gwynne, the house was designed to be 'a real bachelor pad', [1] and is laid out as three octagonal pavilions of blue–brown engineering brick, under shallow pitched roofs of bronze-coloured granular roofing material with black-coated, aluminium window frames. The grouping and the form of the plan relate back, according to Neil Bingham [2], to an earlier 1960s design for Gwynne's long-term patron Bilsby that was made up of three circular pavilions and also to designs for motorway service buildings designed for the M62 at Burtonwood, Cheshire, in the early 1970s. However, equally plausibly, the origin of the design may come from Gwynne's extension

Above: **Manser House, London, UK.** The old kitchen was below the long horizontal windows and consisted of a range of units, including the cooker and sink. In front of this was another range of units providing a worktop or breakfast bar. The kitchen was later moved into the old service rooms that lay behind the pavilion wall to the right of the kitchen area.

Right: **Manser House, London, UK.** Though the interior is now white throughout, in the original design the walls were white under a pine roof and the central pillar or 'island' was brick and pine. The fire hearth and sills throughout the house were made of black slate. The garden aspect of the central pavilion is warmed by an open fire set in the central island, and next to this is the vent for the hot-air central heating system that was popular in the 1970s.

Above: **Manser House, London, UK.** The master bedroom maintains the language of the windows in the rest of the house, with horizontal ones illuminating the bathroom and large, simple picture windows for the bedroom, all with black slate sills.

to the York Theatre Royal of 1967, which features a group of tent-like structures and was the design Bilsby may have been referring to when he asked Gwynne for a house like a tent.[3]

The house was entered through a double-width entrance hall between the first and second pavilions. This gave access on the left to a garage in the lower level of the first pavilion and up to the guest bedroom and bathroom above the garage. To the right was the main pavilion, which formed the core of the house. In the centre of the double-height room was a wide octagonal brick column or 'island' that led up to a timber ceiling. Throughout the house the horizontal surfaces, such as sills, were in black slate.

The design of the main room was ingenious because it was divided into three areas, and this was reflected in the fittings of the central column. On the right, as the room was entered from the hall, was the kitchen with cooking and preparation areas running along the wall under two long thin windows.

Right: **Manser House, London, UK.** To the left of the old kitchen as you enter the central pavilion was the dining area and facing this, in the 'island', is a built-in bar – a Gwynne trademark ever since he began as an architect in the 1930s.

Above: **Manser House, London, UK.** The door handles and locks used throughout the house are from the Modric range by Alan Tye, which by the 1970s had become the default hardware selection for many European and American designers.

Behind this was a work surface and beyond, in the column, was storage for ceramics. To the left of the entrance was the dining table with a bar built into the column and on the farthest, garden, side was an open fireplace in black slate in the column facing a sitting area. The use of the column as a site for built-in elements, like a bar and a fire, is a feature of Gwynne's work that dates back to the 1930s. Between the dining and sitting area was first an entrance down to an inner hall, and then a picture window looking out over the garden. Through the inner hall was a left turn into three utility rooms, while on the right was a door to the patio with its view of the garden. Straight on led to the master bedroom overlooking the garden, with a bathroom to the rear.

When the house was later sold the new owner commissioned Gwynne to alter it by moving the kitchen into the service wing rooms, which were knocked together for the purpose, and adding a long window similar to those over the original site of the kitchen. He also altered the master pavilion by adding another storey so that the bedroom was on the first floor with a study below and, finally, the garage was converted into another bedroom. A further alteration has been to dispense with the masculine language of brick, timber and slate surfaces and to plaster all the surfaces over and paint them white. The garden, though filled with mature trees, was also planted out with small specimen trees and shrubs around a large lawn. This created the effect of a small Victorian arboretum, although the planting followed the modernist garden design methods employed elsewhere on Bilsby's SPAN estates.

1   From interviews between Patrick Gwynne and Neil Bingham, quoted in Neil Bingham, 'The Houses of Patrick Gwynne', *Twentieth Century Architecture*, Issue 4, 2000, p 38.
2   *Ibid*, p 38.
3   See Comment, *ibid*, p 39.

Left: Manser House, London, UK. It is not only the house that is interesting. The garden, front and back, is a good example of the modern British garden of the 1970s with its interest in textures, such as the gravel and granite setts at the front, and colour – for example, the use of many-hued evergreen shrubs at the front and colourful specimen trees at the rear. The house is a series of Brutalist pavilions made of the blue–brown engineering brick that was fashionable in the 1970s, with bronze-coloured roof material contrasted against the lighter colours and textures of the driveway at the front. Windows are given a very abstract treatment and all the voids are defined by black edging. The palette of browns, bronzes and blacks, together with the small windows (except at the rear) is also typical of the 1970s reaction against the use of pale stock brick and white-framed picture windows in the 1960s.

Below: Manser House, London, UK. The front pavilion originally housed a guest bedroom and bathroom over a sunken garage. To the right and set slightly back is the main living area, while the horizontal windows indicate the original position of the kitchen. The rear pavilion was originally a single-storey master bedroom with an *en-suite* bathroom, but this was later altered by Gwynne into a two-storey building with the bedroom and bathroom above a study. Unusually, the large windows of the lower rooms are not full length and, instead, access to the garden is through the hall door between the pavilions.

RECLAIMED

In the United Kingdom restoration has come to mean an almost archaeological exercise of re-creation that at its most extreme simply refers to stabilising the historic fabric of a building like a fly in amber. Elsewhere restoration is considered as a more proactive and creative practice as the Swiss architect Aurelio Galfetti makes clear:

'Restoration, in architecture, is always transformation, because it is true that one restores to conserve but also to respond to new demands, for a new content ... [and] in this sense, restoration is an architectural activity, and the restoration project a project of architecture'.[1]

Galfetti's remarks imply a degree of modification to an old structure and this practice is more akin to creative reclamation, in the sense of winning something back from a wasted condition, than restoration. Until the massive boom in straightforward backward-looking cultural Historicism in the 1980s most projects involving old houses were acts of reclamation or the reuse of old parts integrated with new elements.

Reclaimed

The reclamation of buildings at the level of domestic architecture was an idea that had little currency before the late 1960s and there are few actual examples before the early 1970s. However, by the late 1970s the desire to live in old buildings had outstripped the desire to live in new ones, certainly in countries with a large stock of old houses, like Britain and Italy, or cities like New York. This change of heart had various causes.

One cause was economic, as in the housing markets of the 1970s old buildings were cheaper than new ones and thus attracted the young. Another was scale, because older houses were, by and large, bigger than new ones. Yet another was availability. In Britain, for example, there are still six million Victorian houses, which is many more than the number of modern ones ever built in the UK. Some causes, however, were specific. In Italy, the flooding of Florence in 1966 and the slow sinking of Venice, for example, provided a practical need for reclamation. However, in retrospect, all these pragmatic considerations seem less important than the cultural shifts in attitudes to the architecture of the past that occurred from the mid-1960s onwards and gained general currency in the 1970s.

A good litmus test for this is Terence Conran's *The House Book*, which was first published in 1974 and was in its twelfth printing by 1978. *The House Book* was for the person who, '... although you know what you like, you are not sure how to set about getting it and ... may think it useful, as I do, to analyse the current 'looks' in terms of their main components'.[2] The 'looks' that Conran refers to are, in order of appearance, Farmhouse, Town-house, Country-house, Mediterranean, International and Eclectic. Of these only International is all Modernist, and of this he says: 'This style takes a great deal of skill and money',[3] thereby relegating Modernism to a style and, by

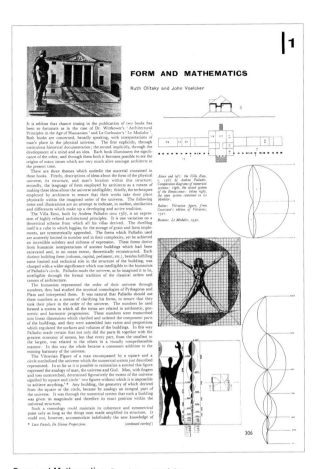

Form and Mathematics. Opening page of the article by Ruth Olitsky and John Voelker, published in *Architectural Design* of October 1954.

implication, one that has passed. Concerning the other styles, they are in the main efforts to make the old a bit more new and the new a bit more old; reclamation rather than renovation or restoration.

As well as the evolution of preservationist movements in Britain in the early 1960s, significant revisions to the understanding of historic buildings also occurred in the architectural profession. This had little to do with preservation and everything to do with new considerations of the purpose of the language of architecture by modern architects. Back in 1954 Olitsky and Voelker, writing in *Architectural Design,* compared two new books: *Wittkower's Architectural Principles in the Age of Humanism* and Le Corbusier's *Le Modulor.*[4] Their conclusion was to suggest that the Modulor and the proportional systems of Palladio were intended for the same purpose, '. . . as part of an intelligible formal language'.[5] Further back, in 1947, Colin Rowe had explored the same territory in his essay 'Mathematics of the Ideal Villa',[6] which was republished in 1976. Writing of this kind began to establish the idea that all good architecture was equivalent and to some degree compatible. In 1966, Venturi published *Complexity and Contradiction in Architecture*[7] which, though often used as a text in support of the deadest Revivalism, was in fact simply a general plea for a psychologically rich architectural language, or typology, that used Baroque and Mannerist architecture as a case study. Venturi also sparked a new interest in understanding why the forms of architecture are as they are and this interest in the language of architecture prompted architects to look at old buildings through new eyes.

At the same time the politicisation of architectural schools and the influence of sociology created an intellectual debate across Europe and America that, among other things, focused on the study of the popular or demotic in architecture. This formed the underlying rationale behind Venturi's *Learning from Las Vegas* (1972)[8] and also Banham's, very different, *Architecture of the Well-tempered Environment* (1969),[9] which traced the history of the development of the ordinary home over the previous century. A further aspect of sociological studies in the 1960s was the growing sense that new technologies were eradicating old ways of life, an idea that framed Jane Jacobs' prescient *The Death and Life of Great American Cities* (1961)[10] and Frampton's later essay on 'critical regionalism' (1983).[11] And all this must be set against the backdrop of an emerging Green movement with its stress on the idea of conserving rather than consuming.

The effect of these debates and the influence of an intellectual culture that was increasingly receptive to ideas of recycling and the validity of the past was to challenge the earlier dominant post-war nostrum that new was best and encourage the idea that the past could be accommodated and used. In architecture there was no particular faction that dominated the reuse of old buildings because this was part of a bigger shift in what Lyotard called the metanarratives of culture away from those of Modernism.[12] However, in the 1970s there was no new metanarrative and so what emerged was a fuzzy and undirected appreciation of the past and its potential in the creation of the new. This new but vague regard for the past in the architectural profession, though it lagged behind that of the public due to architects' investment in Modernism, even found expression in the radical architectural movements of the late 1960s and early 1970s.

Although professing not to understand the term 'language of architecture', the English radical group Archigram produced two projects in 1970 that were in essence about reclaiming old buildings. Addhox Mon Repos Strip and Addhox North Kensington Corner, both by Peter Cook, were riffs on the idea that a style kit could be used to alter the language of typical British homes – in these cases a 19th-century terrace and a 1930s Tudorbethan suburban semi. During 1973, in Italy, the Florentine group Superstudio ran two projects in the Florence School of Architecture – Extra Urban Material Culture and Project Zeno – both of which took as their subject research into disappearing Italian peasant technologies and tools. Elsewhere in Italy and Switzerland academics made extensive inventories of old buildings and the techniques used in their construction, composition and the selection of their sites. This interest in peasant culture also had echoes in the countercultural appreciation of 'sustainable' lifestyles that was the impulse behind many of the experiments in rural communal living that took place in the 1970s, and which form the history of the current New Age movement.

The examples in this section are chosen because they represent different aspects of the vague and undirected, but increasingly significant, reclaiming of old structures that took place in the 1970s. A measure of this is that despite the fact that Superstudio emerged in the anti-restoration culture of Florence in the late 1960s most of the members of the group now do restoration work or are interested in traditional crafts.

The first example, Michael Manser's Capel Manor, is a rigorously Miesian house successfully integrated into a High Victorian site, and it demonstrates the attitude of the late 1960s and early 1970s towards the past in that it reflects the, then current, concept that they could be complementary. A comparable contemporary expression of the idea is found in Kettle's Yard in Cambridge, where Jim Ede's converted cottages, Modern art and Georgian furniture fit seamlessly with Leslie Martin's extension.

In the three examples by Gian Piero Frassinelli there is an attempt to separate the fact of age and the quality of craft from the aura of history. This is an important distinction that separates the reclaimed buildings of the 1970s from the Historicist restorations of the 1980s. Frassinelli became an architect in the politicised atmosphere of the Florence School of Architecture in the 1960s, and underlying his socialist politics was a general dissatisfaction with the way Florence, and by extension Italy, compromised its present to a tourist image of its past. Nonetheless, in his involvement with the Superstudio group Frassinelli explored the demotic crafts and building traditions of Tuscany and other regions. Because of these elements his work combines a respect for craft and local materials with a complete disdain for Historicism of any kind, leading him in the case of his conversion of an apartment on Piazza San Giovanni to create an ultramodern interior in an old building. His reclamations are designed to create new interiors that, while embracing craft, deny Historicism.

Pen-y-Lyn by Christopher Day may not seem to be architecture until one remembers his Architectural Association training and Galfetti's remarks, which were referred to earlier. Day's house represents a rare example of the combination of many different discourses that created a new mindset in the 1970s that continues today. His work is anti-materialist and concerned with quality-of-life issues that are based on a respect for nature, place and leaving a light footprint. His design uses an old building and cheaply available modifications to create a socially flexible space with hierarchy. Leaving aside these 'alternative' considerations, the Day house is in many respects a perfect example of a common British attitude to the country cottage and the reclamation of old buildings, based on the idea that the old is inherently valuable whereas technology, while necessary, is not. An idea best represented at Pen-y-Lyn by the setting of a Raeburn centre stage in the kitchen with the cooker neglected in the background.

The attitude to the use of historic buildings in the 1970s was complex, reflecting the many different new concepts that threatened the hegemony of Modernism. What remained consistent was a progressive attitude to their use, free of the conservative and controlling Reverentialism of the Historicism that emerged in the 1980s.

1   Aurelio Galfetti, 'Conservare = transformare', *Rivista Tecnica* No 12, December 1986. Quoted in Gerardo Brown-Manrique, *The Ticino Guide*, Princeton Architectural Press (Princeton), 1989, p 15.
2   Terence Conran, *The House Book*, Mitchelll Beazley Publishers (London), 1974, p 9.
3   *Ibid*, p 18.
4   Ruth Olitsky and John Voelker, 'Form and Mathematics', *Architectural Design*, October 1954, pp 306–7.
5   *Ibid*, p 307.
6   Colin Rowe, *Mathematics of the Ideal Villa and Other Essays.* MIT Press (Cambridge, MA), 1977.
7   Robert Venturi, *Complexity and Contradiction in Architecture*, MoMA Papers on Architecture, MoMA (New York), 1966.
8   Robert Venturi, Denise Scott-Brown and Steven Izenour, *Learning from Las Vegas*, MIT Press (Cambridge, MA), 1972.
9   Reyner Banham, *Architecture of the Well-tempered Environment*, University of Chicago Press (Chicago, IL), 1969.
10 Jane Jacobs, *The Death and Life of Great American Cities*, Vintage Books (New York), 1961.
11 Kenneth Frampton. 'Towards a critical regionalism: Six points for an architecture of resistance', in Hal Foster (ed) *The Anti-Aesthetic*, Bay Press (Port Townsend, WA), 1983, p 17.
12 Jean-Francois Lyotard, *The Postmodern Condition: A Report on Knowledge*, Manchester University Press (Manchester), 1984.

Capel Manor

Michael Manser

Horsmonden, Kent, UK 1970

Capel Manor stands on a hill in the heart of the Garden of England on the site of a large 19th-century house that covered one-quarter of an acre. Like many other middling-to-large houses of the time, Capel Manor was too big for the reduced needs of the 20th century and lay unoccupied from 1926 until the early 1960s when it was demolished. The house stood on a Renaissance Revival arcaded terrace with a grand staircase leading down to a semiformal garden of herbaceous- and cedar-planted terraces that share an almost Tuscan view across the valley to the downs beyond. Fortunately the terrace, the cedars and the view remained and in 1970 a new house was built that was as luxurious in its indulgent minimalism as the ornate stone decoration of its large predecessor.

The present Capel Manor was designed by Michael Manser Associates as a retreat for a Member of Parliament who wanted a small house but an impressive setting. The gardens cover 5 acres and are a grand and elegant frame to a spectacular view, but this architectural stage on which the new house had to perform was as much a challenge as a gift for the architect since the new design had to complement its setting. A measure of the optimism of the times was the fact that the owner, John Howard, the Conservative MP and secretary to Prime Minister Edward Heath, who might have been expected to erect some kind of neo-mansion, instead opted for a Modernist architect who had built many single-storey, modest-sized homes.

The new Capel Manor is an elegant counterpoint to its setting. A long, low, smoked-glass rectangle standing on a plinth of coarse engineering floor tiles, the house has only two bedrooms and they look out onto a swimming pool surrounded by the architectural remains of an orangery. The design of the house is such that from the dining area, living room, master bedroom and pool there is an uninterrupted view across the garden to the distant silhouette of the church in the hilltop village of Goudhurst. Lawns surround the rest of the house and lead to old, high walls and modern gates that guarantee privacy.

The form of the house evokes the simplicity of Mies' and Johnson's glass-box designs and is full of Miesian regard for the contrast of strength and elegance. The structure is such that two large steel I beams run the length of the building supported by very much smaller, square steel piloti. These beams and supports are set inboard of the line of windows and the windows sit inboard of the roof edge and the plinth exactly below it, thus forming an

Opposite top: **Capel Manor, Kent, UK.** The most striking aspect of the interior design is the translucent pink-and-red striped curtains that entirely cover the glass walls of the house. From outside they give it a constant red colour that is painterly in effect and gives the whole a sculptural quality.

Right and above: **Capel Manor, Kent, UK.** Because of its archetypal simplicity and proportion, the house fits easily into the Classical remains that surround it, like a new Miesian temple among more archaic Pirenesian ruins. The compatibility of Modern and classical architecture, because of their similar aesthetic of simplicity and proportion, was well understood but rarely put into practice on this scale, usually being restricted to the Modernist conversion of interiors of older architecture or the furnishing of new architecture with antiques.

Right: **Capel Manor, Kent, UK.** The lounge is a mixture of British and international features. The blue, semi-engineering brick of the lounge wall and the engineering quarry tiles of the floor were commonly used in British Brutalist architecture at the time. Nothing could be more British than the Baxi underfloor aspirated fireplace and its coal-fire proportions, whereas the sunken living area and the cream shagpile carpet, the floor cushions and the large low rosewood coffee table are very transatlantic, as is the classically proportioned steel frame visible throughout the house.

Opposite: **Capel Manor, Kent, UK.** A great effect of the tinted glazing of the house is that the splendour of the setting is reflected on the outside while remaining visible from visible from inside. This dematerialises the walls so that, although it seems simple, the house's presence is a complex experience – the closer the viewer gets to it the more it seems to disappear.

unsupported veranda around the entire house. Floor-to-ceiling smoked glass, joined at the corners without glazing bars, creates a continuous glazed curtain that is only punctuated by the difference between the panels, which are either fixed or opening, and smaller sections of louvred glass for more controlled ventilation. The tiles of the plinth are the same inside and out, and the same idea is used in the thin varnished planking of the ceiling, into which spotlights are set. The brown tiling of the plinth is picked up in the softer brown of the glass and the roof timber, while the steel beams are painted with chocolate-brown gloss. Inside the plan is very simple. The centre is a large sunken living space running the full width of the house, a rarer form of the split-level rooms that were fashionable at the time. At both ends it is separated from other rooms by a thin wall of exposed, blue, semi-engineering brick. In the middle of one of these are two cavities side by side, one for a 'Baxi' open fire and the other for fuel.

At the end of the house facing the pool are two bedrooms separated by a thin wall, both of which enjoy the complete double aspect of the full-height, glass exterior walls. Between the bedrooms and the living area are two internal bathrooms, lit by skylights, entered by doors facing the garden. Beyond these the living area is entered through an unframed textured glass door. Between the bedrooms and the bathroom on the side facing the pool are built-in cupboards At the other end of the house the kitchen–dining room leads straight off the living area, while on the other side of a dividing wall is a small study or further bedroom. In the kitchen–dining room the kitchen is built into the L of the living room and study walls thus creating a large open area for dining, which still features the Saarinen Tulip dining set that was originally chosen for this area. There is a cellar below the house for storage and utilities, and this is entered by a steep ladder from a door in the centre of the wall opposite the fire. Next to this, behind a matching flush wood door, is more storage including space for drinks and so on.

The house can be entered at a number of points but the main entrance is by the second bedroom, where there is storage for coats built into the second bathroom wall. The building's main spaces are separated by only three doors

made of glass and the entire exterior is glass. The only areas that are enclosed and have conventional doors are the bathrooms and the entrance to the cellar. Heating is provided through vents at the foot of the curtain window. The windows of the house feature the translucent drapes, in the same pattern throughout, that were used in the original furnishing scheme and which are hung from a continuous track attached to the ceiling. These, when closed, combined with the semireflective smoked glass have the effect of reflecting the garden in the glass making it impossible to see into the house. The windows' partial internal reflections remain with the curtains open and thus at all times the house borrows the garden for some of its architectural effect.

The principal effect of the house through its complete curtain glazing and absence of spaces, bar the bathrooms, without panoramic views, or indeed any space really separated from any other, is to unify the exterior with the interior. This, combined with the reflective effects of the glazing, creates the sense that the building hovers on the edge of intangibility, as from within and without the old garden washes over and through the new house. The result is so successful because although the geometric purity of the design is very assertive, and thus has a very definite character, its low profile and reflective medium neither dominate the terrace, as the old Capel Manor once did, nor impose on the garden or the view, both of which were the cause of the building of the new house. Manser's minimalist design reclaims the old garden without really altering its old form, and this move towards a respect forcontext and accommodation of pre-existing forms was a new feature in 1970s architecture, very much in marked contrast to the *tabula rasa* Modernism of the previous decade.

Casale Fontibucci

Gian Piero Frassinelli

Bagno a Ripoli, Florence, Italy   1970

Gian Piero Frassinelli graduated in architecture in 1968 and joined the Florence-based radical architectural group Superstudio in the same year. The theoretical position of the group and his practice were both products of the city of Florence and its School of Architecture, and this was a complex and often conflicted position, particularly in its attitudes to the crafts, restoration and modern architecture. On the one hand they espoused a contempt for the stultifying reverential attitude to its past that hung over Florentine culture and choked any genuine newness, while on the other hand they displayed an interest in the problem of modernising the old and were attracted to the genuine craft traditions of the Tuscan working classes. Despite this complex internal position, Frassinelli's architecture has a coherence and direction that stands apart from his polemical cultural interventions with Superstudio.

His work on houses reveals a regard both for the vernacular traditions of Italy and, more importantly, for their materials and crafts. It is this regard for the methods of the past as opposed to its forms that has enabled Frassinelli to restore the old and integrate it with the unashamed new, free from any intimidated respect for historical precedent.

In 1970 Frassinelli restored the modest Renaissance buildings of Casale Fontibucci, the new home of his sister and, by repute, originally the home of Michelangelo's stonemason. The site of the house lies on a hill commanding a view down the valley of the Arno to Florence in the distance past the picturesque array of hilltop palazzi and villas in between.

The main problems of the Casale Fontibucci were the decay of the original stonework and the darkness of the interior inherent in the design of old agricultural buildings. The first problem was solved by identifying the clay-stone from which the house was built. Remarkably, this involved Frassinelli reopening the original and now abandoned quarry that the soft stone came from and finding a mason able to use it correctly. The second problem was that the house was dark at its centre because of its wide square plan and few small windows; this was dealt with in a different manner that was modern and without regard for history. Since Frassinelli's original restoration work the building has been modified gradually over the years, so the description here is of what remains of his original work.

The original building was an old farmhouse with the ground floor functioning as a barn and the first floor as a house accessed by an external flight of stairs. Frassinelli unified the two by inserting a large internal stairwell at the centre of the rear wall. Next to this he built an arcaded corner entrance to the house made up of one wide, shallow Romanesque arch on each wall

Above: **Casale Fontibucci, Florence, Italy.** The house is in part restoration and in part modernisation. The architect reopened the old quarry that the stone for the early 16th-century house came from and repaired some damaged areas, but also opened up some others, notably the doorway on the upper floor and the arches of the hall on the ground floor. The old windows and doors are clearly visible, and from these it can be deduced how dark the original house was.

Opposite: **Casale Fontibucci, Florence, Italy.** To bring light into the building the architect created a glazed atrium that extends along the upper entrance passage to the centre of the house, where a room-sized stairwell was made. Next to this area, on the upper floor, the architect inserted a glass pyramid to form a very high roof to the bathroom, creating a dramatic interior without altering the wall fenestration. The bathroom has since had a false roof inserted below th pyramid because of problems with the double glazing.

Right: **Casale Fontibucci, Florence, Italy.** The entrance hall opens onto the stairwell atrium of the house through a glass wall that repeats the trademark Superstudio grid used outside, and shows the effectiveness of the device as a means of bringing in light and, *inter alia,* changing the feel of the house from that of a peasant structure to that of a palazzo.

Above: **Casale Fontibucci, Florence, Italy.** The toilet and upper atrium share the architect's concern to create internal spaces that do not relate to the outside world, while the tiling in the toilet shows the flexibility of the Superstudio grid motif, which can function almost as a brand.

Opposite: **Casale Fontibucci, Florence, Italy.** The 'flying' staircase of the atrium is typical of the anti-historicist stance of Superstudio – conscious industrial styling surrounded by old stone. In the original design bamboo created a forest around the stairs, but this caused problems with vermin and was replaced by less overwhelming signifiers of exotic growth which frame some of the owner's collection of African art.

meeting at the corner. This entrance area was made into a lobby glazed on three sides, two external and one internal glass wall giving onto the stairwell. He made the stairs from two short runs that turned on a half-landing, all constructed of steel and suspended so that they only touched the building at the bottom and the top. The upper landing was made from the old house's entrance hall that led from the external stair. This area was made lighter by fully glazing the entrance right up to the roof and continuing this along the old entrance-passage roof to the new light-well, and here too the roof area is totally glazed. The effect of the whole is to create what would now be called an atrium. The rooflights were constructed from trapezoidal and pyramidal glazed forms and another pyramid was used to glaze the roof of the bathroom, creating a massive, high, top-lit room.

The intervention of the entrance hall and the internal atrium for the stairs and old entrance hall are uncompromisingly contemporary forms in an old shell, symbolised at roof level by massive areas of glazing in large geometric forms. Frassinelli wished to signal his modern forms very clearly and throughout he used grey steel as his construction material and signifier. On the exterior fenestration of the new areas, and on the interior glass wall of the entrance hall, the architect used a tight-squared grid that is analogous to the small-squared grid that formed the module for Superstudio's plans and objects. Though the reference to his radical Superstudio practice is clear, the grid form is also an almost iconic element in the typology of Florentine palazzi fenestration. It is hard to imagine this historic reference was unintentional here and simply a reference to the established Superstudio trademark, and it is equally unlikely that it is a politically motivated ironic Superstudio gesture, since the house was a project for a family member.

Apartment on Piazza San Giovanni

Gian Piero Frassinelli

Piazza San Giovanni, Florence, Italy   1974

More political tension is found in another conversion of an old building, but this time one set in the highly culturally significant site of Piazza San Giovanni overlooking the baptistry of the Duomo, the entrance facade of the Duomo and Giotto's campanile next to it. This is the epicentre of the arguments that raged in the Florence architectural community over the proper response to the problems of preservation, modernisation and the self-image of the city. There could almost be no better site for a Superstudio project or opportunity for a Situationist-style intervention.

In 1974 Frassinelli was commissioned to convert an apartment in a late 19th-century building, almost at the intersection of the contiguous Piazza San Giovanni and Piazza del Duomo. The client wanted the most uncompromising up-to-date design, although this would be invisible from the exterior which would remain a typical city-centre Beaux-Arts block.

The apartment was on the top floor of the building and this was used by Frassinelli to create more height and space by adapting Le Corbusier's plan for the Pavilion de l'Esprit Nouveau (1925) with its use of double-height living space and a mezzanine. Although it had the conventionally high ceiling of a 19th-century Italian building, the apartment had a shallow roof. While it was possible to create a mezzanine in the principal living area by having a low ceiling height below the mezzanine and by opening up the ceiling above to the roof, the height gained in the main part of the room was not very appreciable. This was because the existing ceiling met the roofline at the cornice of the building and would have only gained a metre and a half at the apex of the roof, which in any case lay over the proposed mezzanine.

To achieve the extra height in the living area Frassinelli used the device of a grid, inserted at the level of the old ceiling, that extended to the edge of the mezzanine where it was at waist height. At this point it was joined to the mezzanine by bars that continued the grid motif, forming a balustrade for the open mezzanine. The grid was divided into closed oblong sections over the main living area, and open square sections at the intersection of the grid and mezzanine. The sections above the living area were closed with mirrored glass panels, creating the sense of height required but with the surreal effect of reflecting the contents of the room below.

The mezzanine is accessed by an open spiral staircase with pressed steel treads, placed between the kitchen area under the mezzanine and the living area. It enters the mezzanine through the floor rather than adjacent to it so as not to interfere with the effect of the mirrored ceiling. The kitchen is on the one hand an unremarkable arrangement of built-in units around the wall, with a bar across its width to separate it from the living area. However, on the other

Private Apartment, Florence, Italy. Superstudio had a problematic relationship with their Italian architectural past, which they felt made it difficult for a city like Florence to have a present. Where a contemporary architect would probably try to enhance the view of the nearby baptistry, Frassinelli reduced its presence by the creation of a severe industrial frame for the ancient structure beyond.

hand, it is actually a very assertive, almost submarine-like statement of modernity. The ceiling is made up of pressed steel-units fitted between a central supporting I beam, and all the surfaces are painted in a gloss aquamarine–turquoise blue with the exception of the floor and the worktops, which are black. The space is illuminated by very thin fluorescent lights set in the gaps between the pressed-steel ceiling panels. This vivid blue is also used for the floors of the mezzanine, the frames of the ceiling mirrors, the mezzanine baluster and the framing of the windows. The windows were originally set in floor-to-ceiling recesses and these have been filled in with steel panels and the windows reduced to a recessed square casement, also made of steel. Below the windows, radiators are boxed in behind perforated-steel sheets.

By comparison with the kitchen–living area the rest of the apartment is fairly conventional, being made up of two bedrooms with fitted furniture and *en-suite* bathrooms. Throughout, there is an almost subterranean feeling that was common in 1970s urban conversions, created by a combination of obscured windows, low levels of spotlighting and the contrast of shiny and velvet textured surfaces. This last effect is used in the bedrooms, of which one, the master bedroom, has the most original décor of a bed set on a plinth with the wall at its head covered in a contrasting dark, textured material. The other bedroom is painted in a then fashionable Art Deco cream throughout. Though the apartment now feels like a time capsule, in part because of its wealth of original features and famous furniture designs, when it was first completed it was a statement of the utmost modernity; a Superstudio attack on the stultifying Historicism of Florence.

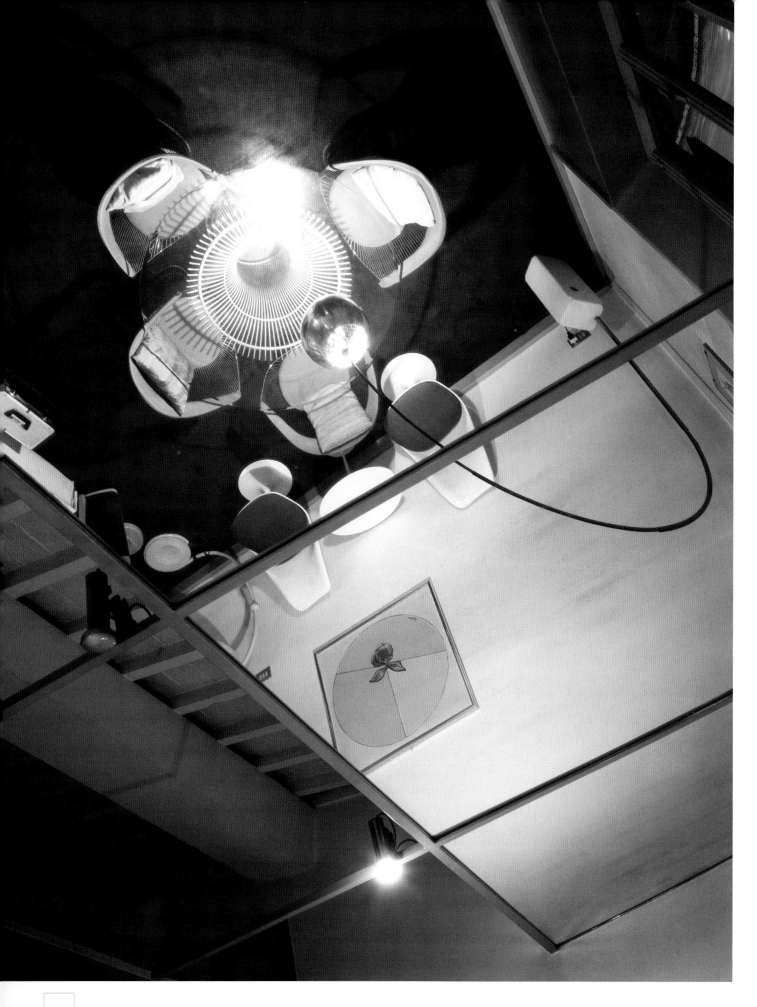

This self-conscious, anti-historical modernity gives a rationale for the devices used to isolate the apartment from the shell that surrounds it, and for the use of such ahistorical and industrial materials as steel and blue gloss paint. The apartment seems to epitomise the political position of Superstudio in its early phase, and is almost like a political gesture undertaken in collaboration with the owner; a piece of stealth contemporaneity at the heart of a world heritage site. However, while being a good example of a Superstudio gesture, this apartment is uncharacteristic of Frassinelli's work, which more usually shows an interest in, and sensitivity to, the natural materials and craft traditions of old buildings.

Right: **Private Apartment, Florence, Italy.**
The furniture and decoration of the living room are original, with the sofa and low glass-topped coffee table, the cream walls and mahogany carpet all typical of the glamorous contemporary Italian styling of designers like Vico Magistretti. While the Castiglioni Arco floor lamps (1962) and an American Platner dining set (1966) date from the 1960s, their baroque styling is in keeping with the more flamboyant 1970s.

Opposite: **Private Apartment, Florence, Italy.**
To increase the apparent height of the room and thereby create the sense of double-height space, the architect inserted a mirrored ceiling at the old soffit level above the living area, creating a strangely alienating effect – one used extensively in architecture during the 1970s, but not usually in living rooms.

Casa Fabi

Gian Piero Frassinelli
Cernobbio, Como, Italy   1975

Lake Como lies at the foot of the Alps on the Italian side of the Swiss border, and has the special character of being a long and narrow lake with two forks forming a Y-shape. Being sheltered between mountains and lying to the south-east of the mass of the Alps, it has a subtropical climate. At its most southerly point lies the ancient city of Como, about 40 kilometres north of Milan. As well as having a long cultural history of its own and a long-established silk industry, since the 19th century Como and its lake have long been resorts for wealthy Milanese. Much of the land around the lake is given over to a succession of elegant villas of every period, and these have overwhelmed the ancient villages that surround the lake so that they combine picturesque centres and luxurious villa-rich suburbs. Cernobbio, very near Como, is both a charming village by the lake and a luxury suburb of Como, filled with large mansions set in subtropical gardens of exotic trees and lush plants.

Many of these grand houses have long since been divided into apartments, and the Casa Fabi occupies the top floor of a late 19th-century villa in an opulent interpretation of an Alpine theme replete with timbers, frescoed plaster infills and an overreaching roofline. The owner, a business-woman in the Como silk trade, commissioned Frassinelli to convert the attic into an apartment linked to another that she also owned below. While the lower floor retains much of its original form, the empty attic enabled him to create a luxurious open space that has a particular 1970s opulence and represents a complete synthesis of Frassinelli's interests in vernacular technologies and creating modern living spaces.

The fundamental problem with the attic was its shallow roof and lack of headroom, so Frassinelli dropped its floor to the top of the windows on the floor below. This had the effect of creating enough height at the centre of the apartment to make the whole area feel spacious and airy. The extra height at the walls of the new space to enabled him to create a discreet roof terrace at one corner of the floor area. This was achieved by cutting back the roof to the structural joists of the main support beams, which were then braced by an offset metal post so as not to interrupt the sense of openness of the terrace.

The next major intervention into the floor area was the creation of a large entrance stair turning on a half-landing that terminates in a fully glazed entrance hall below. This glamorous entrance was made more so by the use of a radiused glazed wall fitted into the rectangular space of the stairwell which, with the completely glass entrance hall below, creates a sense of entering a space of absolute modernity from a historical building. To add to the sense of height, and hence drama, of the wide entrance Frassinelli

Above: **Casa Fabi, Como, Italy.** The entrance to the apartment has to make the transition between the conventional spaces of the main body of the building and the wide-open spaces of the attic. This is achieved by making the entrance large, open and well lit, which is in contrast to the darkness usually associated with attics. The stairs are also designed in a contemporary mode, with a steel staircase radiused on the half-landing and cased in plate glass, so that they are visibly separated from the old building within which they are placed.

Right: **Casa Fabi, Como, Italy.** The most significant feature of the apartment is the exposed wooden roof, which was simply cleaned and left exposed. The architect's decision to do this, rather than plaster it over, derives from his interest in traditional techniques and structures created by artisan builders, which is a reflection of his social-ist political position. in his other projects, where there is a large intervention into the structure. this is made without reference to context and is assertively modern. Here the roof terrace is made from a cutout in the roof enclosed by metal-framed double-glazing. The cutting of the roof made extra support necessary, and this is added in the most functional and undisguised way.

Above: **Casa Fabi, Como, Italy.** The design of the lower apartment is much more restrained than that of the attic, but it retains the architect's principal design device of seeking to separate the interior from any sense of being linked to the Historicist building within which it is situated. In this case the separation is created by the inner windows, which create the sense of a building within a building.

Opposite: **Casa Fabi, Como, Italy.** To create enough height in the attic to be able to stand at its perimeter, the floor had to be lowered to the tops of the windows on the floor below. Other than from the roof terrace, there are no clear views from the apartment because it was not permitted to alter the exterior below roof level. The architect made a virtue of both these pragmatic conditions of the design by creating a logical continuation of the fenestration of the floors below in the roof-lights of the attic, and opening the floor up so that light from the windows on the floor below can come up under the skylights.

carried the side walls up into the eaves of the attic. This device enabled him to create a closed bathroom and kitchen on each side of the entrance hall. Otherwise the space is undivided except for a massive stone cross wall in the centre of the attic, but this only extends halfway across the space. The wooden roof was cleaned of dirt but otherwise left in its original state, and the stone walls were either cleaned and left exposed or harled to create an alternate rhythm of textures that are taken from the exterior finish of the building.

The plan of the apartment is simple. Entering from the stairs and turning right, there is a short corridor created by the exposed stone cross wall and the wall of the bathroom. This corridor gives onto a large double bedroom and *en-suite* bathroom. Retracing one's steps and coming back to the stairs and looking into the open space of the attic, there is in the far right corner a raised wooden platform. A short flight of stairs leads out through double glass doors fitted into a steel-framed glass wall that leads to the roof terrace with its chest-height parapet. Re-entering the main space and looking across the room to the other side, the space is divided up into a sitting area with low sofas, armchairs and a coffee table, while directly in front and to the left of this is a long dining table in front of a waist-height, metre-wide open fire. To the left of this are a bamboo and bird's-eye maple serving and storage area, designed by Frassinelli, and then a door into a galley kitchen. Frassinelli also designed the solid-wood table made up of four modules.

One of the restrictions on the design was that the exterior fenestration could not be altered, so that from the outside the house looks unaltered. The original windows to the attic were only narrow openings just below the eaves, primarily to let in enough air and light to allow the space to be used for storage. Frassinelli increased the light levels by introducing skylights, set low in the roof just above where it meets the walls of the house. These were placed above the windows of the floor below wherever possible. Thus, in the main

living–dining area there are skylights set in pairs at the corners of the room, except where the roof terrace is situated. In the bedroom there are shuttered skylights at the outside corners of the room, and there are also skylights in the galley kitchen and in the bathroom. Frassinelli also used the lowered floor to provide floor-level windows in the living–dining area by borrowing light from the long windows of the room below through the simple device of cutting an aperture in the lower part of the wall above the window and in the floor that adjoins it. These floor lights are exactly below the skylights and create very dramatic lighting effects that, together with the roof terrace, compensate for the lack of views from the apartment windows.

As in the case of the apartment on Piazza San Giovanni, Frassinelli creates a sense of separation from the rest of the historic villa through removing any sense of its presence. In the case of the Casa Fabi, once you enter the hall the views are entirely internal, with the exception of the terrace. Because of this lack of exterior, Frassinelli has emphasised space and freedom of movement by the preservation of a sense of complete openness in the apartment – even the bedroom, though isolated behind the cross wall, has no door. He also used the roof structure and the textures of the walls, combined with equally dramatic natural lighting, to create a changing internal landscape articulated by changing light conditions outside.

Casa Fabi, Como, Italy. The servery is made from bamboo with bird's-eye-maple veneered drawer units and a marble worktop. This combination of exotic and highly figured materials is in keeping with the work of many Italian furniture designers of the mid-1970s, and reflects the international taste for Art Deco glamour, making this a surprising design for an architect usually determinedly Modern.

Casa Fabi, Como, Italy. The bathroom shows Frassinelli's great ability to imbue architectural spaces with an abstract sculptural quality, in this case through the wall treatments and the use of very simply styled equipment. The liquid figuring of the marble in the kitchen gives the wall a sense of depth in a very constricted space. In the bathroom, the treatment of the hexagonal tiling reduces a sense of enclosure in the shower area by creating a less rigid demarcation between spaces than would normally be the case with straight-edged tiles.

In the conversion of the apartment below, made as a result of the lowering of its ceiling, Frassinelli has been much less intrusive adding only a spiral stair of the type used in his apartment on Piazza San Giovanni to create an internal access to the apartment in the attic, and altering the glazing so that the openings in the floor of the attic apartment do not intrude in any way on the people in the apartment below. This has been achieved by the insertion of a second layer of glazing on the inside edge of the window aperture.

This apartment has no apparent relation to the Superstudio project that can be seen in Frassinelli's Florentine work, but it does relate to projects at the architecture school in Florence, where he collaborated with Superstudio members who were concerned to document disappearing peasant technologies and design techniques. In one of these, Project Zeno, the idea was to study a Tuscan peasant farmer, Zeno, and his life. This research revealed that Zeno had totally rebuilt a bentwood chair in the process of dozens of repairs that he made to it over a period of 50 years. This has some deep resonances in Frassinelli's work, which seems at its most sensitive and inventive in reclaiming old buildings; the ingenious use of pre-existing forms seems to suit his architecture more naturally than the positional practices of his Superstudio activities.

Pen-y-Lyn

Christopher Day

Crymych, Pembrokeshire, UK 1975–1997

Pen-y-Lyn lies just off the old-fashioned, two-lane road that crosses the Preseli Mountains from Haverfordwest to Cardigan, at the point where the small fields of the lowland farms give way to the unhedged open moor of the mountains. A crossroads marks the turn and if you go the wrong way you soon come to Pentre Ifan, a Bronze Age tomb 4000 years old made from a massive slab of stone improbably supported by three slender stone posts.

The house lies at the end of a muddy track bounded by deep mossy walls, ash trees and bracken. Beyond it the onward direction of the walls ends and well-made turns take them away, right and left, to mark the edge of farmed land. Ahead there is the tussocky grass of the moor, which eventually gives way to rocks and heather below the ragged crest of the hills. To the right a stream curves around a lush gully that passes the side of Pen-y-Lyn. Between the stream and the end wall of this long house is a small sheltered vegetable garden. Walking along the front of the building, back towards the track, a tiny house lies on the other side of the path, up by the end wall of the larger one, by the track and opposite an old wooden barn.

Both structures are the work of the New Age architect Christopher Day. The long stone house dates back to the 1750s and was originally a barn. The other is a tiny two-roomed, two-storey building, one room per floor. Originally a pigsty, it has been extended upwards to another floor but large windows and whitewashed walls make the space seem larger, like a Carthusian retreat for the digital age.

The architect began converting the long house in 1975, and the process continued until the 1990s when he became too disabled to work on the site any more. To understand the building and its almost organic growth it has to be walked around rather than considered facade by facade. The front wall of the house retains its traditional one-and-a-half-height walls under a slate roof and its small, well-spaced windows, which date back to its original purpose as a barn. The furthest end wall has had new window apertures put into what was a blank wall and, following the Steineresque attitude to space of the architect, these have irregularly headed casements in dark-stained wood.

The rear of the house, facing south up to the moor, has an irregular range of lean-to constructions that run its length. The earliest of these, at the west end, has a slate roof with skylights and solar panels over conventional stone walling. The larger, later, eastern lean-to has a continuous course of mullioned fenestration over a stone wall, to waist height under corrugated, asbestos-type sheet roofing. Above this extension the wall of the old barn has been lowered to allow a continuous run of mullions under the roofline, and the room terminates in a balcony at the east end-wall of the house, with stairs up from

the ground. Next to these the east lean-to ends in half-walls under windows to each side of a half-glazed door, all of which fit directly under the shallow-angled corrugated roof.

As with the majority of the house's fittings all the added windows and extensions are custom-made in an effective but low-tech manner. This enhanced DIY aesthetic gives a clue to the essence of Day's approach, which combines the concern of the 1970s artist with the process of making being the art in art and the view that what we build for ourselves is our major artwork: 'Almost everywhere . . . the charm of a place is due to human activity'[1] . . . 'Our surroundings are potentially the most powerful artform we experience in our lives'.[2] Equally, he is instinctively against regularity in the tradition of Steiner and even Archigram: 'It may be ridiculous to make every window different just for the sake of being different, but it is even more so to make every one the same just for the sake of being the same, or to shape them just to impose an elevational pattern.'[3]

The interior of the house combines the spatial complication and strangely logical coherence of the organically developed space. The materials are a simple palette of slate floors, whitewashed stone walls, natural redwood pine and plastered ceilings with exposed joists or bracings.

The house can be entered through half-glazed doors at several points: the front door in the middle of the mostly unaltered front elevation; the back door into the kitchen towards the west end of the lean-to range; the architect's bedroom in the middle of the lean-to range; the architect's office through the east end-wall of the lean-to range; and, finally, the easternmost bedroom via

Pen-y-Lyn, Pembrokeshire, UK. In the bathroom the modern bath and shower are moderated by their dark hue and the décor of the room, with its rough whitewashed walls, irregular window and use of slates around the bathroom fittings where ceramic tiles would more conventionally appear.

the stairs up to its balcony. These combine to give the house a general permeability entirely in keeping with the anti-structural beliefs of the architect, and are indicative of the complete lack of hierarchy of spaces inside where there are few traditional continuities.

Beginning at the entrance to the architect's office next to the track, this room then narrows into a passage leading back to the west end. Off the passage to the right is a small sky-lit bathroom for the architect who can no longer go upstairs. Its fittings are default DIY white with standard, low-cost taps, but the irregular walls and sky-lit whitewash give it a homely cottage familiarity with a hippy spin that is present in every room and seems to be what the architect means when he talks of the need for buildings to have soul. Opposite is his bedroom, a brightly lit, low-ceilinged room that looks up to the mountains to the south. Beyond this is the larder–kitchen–dining area in the form of a long room entered from three points: at the east end from the architect's rooms and at the midpoint through two doors, one from the garden and another opposite from the rest of the house. The layout of this area next to a suite for the architect to work and sleep in minimises the impact of his disability on the lives of the family, as he is never more than a few metres from everything that he needs or the normal spaces and interactions of family life. The kitchen is a very conventional British conception of the centre of the home. High ceilings above a redwood pine food-storage and preparation area at one end with a large, bench-surrounded table that just fits into the other end, the whole arranged around a white Raeburn in the centre of the room.

Pen-y-Lyn, Pembrokeshire, UK. The large east bedroom of the house is also configured as a workspace. Though the need for individual private areas for each member of a household was a recommendation of the Parker Morris report in the early 1960s, it was not until the 1970s that bedrooms began to be treated as more than service areas for the family rooms of a house.

Through a handmade, half-glazed, irregularly semicircular topped door is a small open area leading to stairs up and a small living room to the front. This room is a beamed, low-ceilinged space featuring the other great domestic icon of the cottage – an inglenook – except that here the fireplace is a home-made hearth that is like a hybrid of a stove, a fireplace and a bread oven. To the rear of the room two more curved-top doors lead into bedrooms, one facing north and the other south, both with a double aspect. Each is furnished with a double bed on a pine divan fitted into the end of the room under the windows, and built-in pine shelving near the doors. On the kitchen side of the sitting room, on the side of the inglenook, a door leads to another living room with a double aspect through small windows.

Returning to the centre of the house where all the access points to the house converge, a sky-lit stair leads up to a half-landing where it splits east and west. To the west is the rear upstairs bedroom which, like its eastern counterpart, has a long run of timber-mullioned windows under the eaves looking up at the mountainside. The room is the full width of the house. The other stairway leads to a bathroom with a dark chocolate-brown basin and bath under white walls. But the bathroom is only a passage because to its rear, heading north, is the entrance to a narrow corridor that passes through built-in shelves holding the architect's records and other family belongings and gives onto the eastern bedroom with its run of mountain-facing windows and the balcony at the east end. This, too, is the full width of the house and passing out onto the balcony and down its stairs brings one back to the entrance door to the architect's office.

Throughout the house it is noticeable that the architect has retained the old 'front' facade in its original form, with few windows and only on the ground floor. Thus, the house you arrive at is a mid 18th-century building. But at the end wall and in all the 'rear' of the house every effort has been made to give all the rooms where people take their leisure – the bedrooms, bathroom, office and dining area – as much light and as many vistas of the Preseli Mountains as possible. The front rooms with their dark diffused light are made to feel cosy by low ceilings and the close-by micro landscape of the flora-rich banks of the earth-covered stone wall only a few metres away.

The architect has exploited the natural setting of the house to provide two contrasting domestic environments: large well-lit spaces with long views, and a smaller more intimate environment of enclosed and cosy spaces. In doing this he has also captured the spirit of the original barn and the view that attracted him to the site originally. It is this approach, where the *genius loci* is recognised as much in the old vernacular structures as in the place itself, that informed the architect's interest in the idea of reinhabiting old buildings.

The architecture here is one that seeks to address intangible quality-of-life issues that in previous decades had been approached from the position that there could be a technological fix to them. Day's and others' concern to cosset the spirit is the architect's response to the introspective counterculture of the early 1970s, which also found its expression in the taste for cottage kitchens and Aga culture that still has currency now. Where his work goes beyond this formulaic comfort zone is in his embrace of the ethos of flexibility, permeability and growth that has its roots in the fine art culture of the 1960s and early 1970s, and which also influenced urban architecture, Archigram and the Metabolists.

1   Christopher Day, *Places of the Soul: Architecture and Environmental Design as a Healing Art*. HarperCollins (London), 1990.

2   *Ibid.*

3   *Ibid.*

HISTORICIST

A comparison between new, architect-built houses of the 1960s and those of the 1970s would show a strong aesthetic influence taken from historical styles in the houses of the 1970s. This Historicism increased markedly in the 1980s in Britain and America, in line with the neo-conservative politics of that decade, and a complete retreat from Modernism is apparent in the work of British architects like Robert Adam, and Quinlan Terry whose Richmond Riverside development in London (1986–8) was no less than an attempt to re-create 18th-century architecture. Equally, communities like the Poundsbury Estate in Dorchester (1988), planned by the Luxembourg architect Léon Krier, and Seaside at Santa Rosa in Florida (1982), planned by Miami property developer Robert Davis, tried to re-create older community structures using local architectural vernaculars in an attempt to deny the 20th century.

Historicist

Between the Modernist anti-Historicism of the 1960s and the revivalism of the 1980s stand the 1970s, where the argument between Modernism and Historicism was first played out. The twin aspects of Historicism that define this debate are the local historical styles bound up in the term vernacular and the international transcultural Historicism implied in the term Classicism. In general, it is possible to say that the Historicism evident in the 1970s began with a reassessment of the vernacular and concluded with a re-examination of the aesthetics of Classicism.

A renewed interest in vernacular architecture was apparent in Britain in the late 1960s and early 1970s, but this was not so much an interest in exterior appearance as a concern with social structure that had developed out of sociological worries about the effects of mass-housing schemes, new towns and housing policies that dismantled and relocated populations. Architects, planners and sociologists began to look at the structures of the societies dismantled under slum clearance and reconstruction schemes, and from the re-evaluation emerged a new understanding of the architectural signifiers of belonging. In terms of architecture this work initially resulted in attempts to humanise mass housing by devices like the 'streets in the air' that were a feature of Alison and Peter Smithson's Robin Hood Gardens estate in London (1972) or re-creating architectural informality through the irregular housing elevations and road patterns that were a prominent feature of the *Essex Design Guide for Residential Areas* (1973).[1] Even Archigram had begun to look at the idea of reusing old structures to create hybrid modern–old living environments in Peter Cook's ADDHOX from Archigram 9 (1970). Equally, critics like Reyner Banham were moving away from a wholehearted support for Modernism towards a newer position that favoured smaller architecture fitted to local context.

In the emergent counterculture of the late 1960s there was a deep suspicion of almost all the technological positivist nostrums of the older reconstruction generation, including Modernist architects and planners, and a new appreciation of small-scale, localised, non-industrial cultures, and this generated a renewed interest in the crafts and their architectural equivalent – the vernacular. In Britain the earliest architectural manifestations of this were in public housing projects like Darbourne and Darke's Pimlico estate (1975), which referenced London's Victorian vernacular through irregular brick elevations, and Horsburgh's Long Acre estate, which referenced the dense urban street plan of alleys and courts found in the Covent Garden area.

In the private housing market the reappropriation of the vernacular, which began in the mid-1960s, was initially based on no more than a wistful urban romanticism about things rural and found its expression in the rehabilitation of old buildings for weekend cottages. However, by the 1970s there emerged a much more widespread re-evaluation of Georgian and Victorian urban domestic architecture as the moderately wealthy began to reinhabit the largely late-Georgian and Victorian inner-city suburbs.

This revival in the taste for past styles among the middle classes was more important than it may seem because it marked the emergence in architecture of values that had hitherto adhered to fashion. While some architects and clients were genuinely interested in traditional architecture, for many the appearance of a building was being disassociated from its function because this was possible with new technology. Earlier in the century living in a vernacular building meant living at an old standard unless you were very rich, but by the early 1970s old buildings could reflect the latest tastes and technologies inside.

The vernacular revival of the early 1970s was happy to combine warm modern kitchens and bathrooms with antique furnishings and 'traditional' exteriors. This approach to historic architecture is most common in Britain and America, both in serious attempts to learn from the skills of the past, as is the case with the Johnston House at Longburgh in Cumbria, and in more aesthetically driven designs, which use the vernacular to create superlocal buildings. These are not only free from the conventions of Modernist aesthetics, because of their basis in vernacular language, but also free of historical restrictions, through the application and use of modern technology – as is the case with Jaffe's Perlbinder House, which applied a seigneurial scale to a typology of building associated with a basic rural existence.

In continental Europe the use of Historicism in the architecture of the 1970s was more complex. In many countries there was, and remains, a commitment not just to new but to Modernist architecture as an expression of cultural positivism. However, in the mid-1960s a new architectural position began to emerge in northern Italy and the Italian-speaking Swiss canton of Ticino. This new position, initially laid out in Aldo Rossi's *The Architecture of the City* (1966),[2] proposed a method of analysing architecture in a manner that fully explored its relation to site, history, man and the evolution of architectural forms. In doing this Rossi was entering into a critique of the kind of Modernist architecture and planning, which regarded the historical city as a problem, that had its heyday from the late 1930s to the 1940s.

Rossi posited the historical city as a source of inspiration in a manner that had some parallels with Venturi's 1966 reappraisal of Italian Mannerist and

Baroque architecture, *Complexity and Contradiction in Architecture*.[3] Unlike Venturi, Rossi was also concerned to establish a scientific and contextually sensitive set of tools for the analysis of the city and, by extension, all architecture. This set of tools, particularly the idea that very detailed study should be made of individual building types, their setting and relation to other types, brought about a series of academic architectural projects, some long term, in Italy and Ticino that were in effect very detailed studies of previously unconsidered local vernaculars. Though Rossi's writing was an attack on Modernism it did not propose Historicism as an antidote: rather, it proposed a more considered and evolutionary approach to architecture that should be open to the lessons of previous architectures.

This approach, which became termed Rationalism, offered a way out of the restrictions of the Modernist aesthetic. Its effects can be seen in the 1970s architecture of Ticino in a number of different forms. For Luigi Snozzi the study of Ticinese village architecture altered the site and orientation of his Modernist designs, whereas a similar interest in local architecture had a different effect on Mario Botta. As Tita Carloni, for whom Botta once worked as an assistant, writes: 'Mario Botta's constructional revolution has other roots, substantially. One is certainly to be found in the silent lessons of peasant architecture in the pre-Alpine valleys and the Po valley, based essentially on the solid wall (of stone or brick) and the great covered voids

Tonini House, Ticino, Switzerland. Modernist in its use of materials and Palladian in its massing and proportions, the Tonini House is all the more remarkable for its ability to look the part of a palazzo while occupying an ordinary suburban plot in an undistinguished but pleasant village outside Belinzona, Ticino. Though clearly Historicist, Reichlin and Reinhart's design is regarded by local architectural critics as referencing the vernacular of the pre-Alpine and northern Italian regions. The interior contains an early example of the now ubiquitous atrium, which functions as the dining room in a return to pre-Modern formality.

(porticoes, lofts, the great threshing hearths) where protection is the aim rather than enclosure.'[4]

At first glance Mario Botta's Casa Bianchi seems at one level to emerge as a fully formed new architectural aesthetic. Its monolithic tower structure of concrete blocks and its apparent windowlessness combined with its red steel, industrial bridge of an entrance goes beyond Modernist Brutalism towards the Post-Modernism of his later work. But seen in context it has a clear relation to the small tower houses with large open belvederes of the nearby village architecture. Botta's interest in the Ticinese historic vernacular and the massive simplicity of agricultural buildings can also be seen in a house he built in Maggia in 1967, which clearly takes its inspiration from a typological study of local buildings in both its material and form.

Botta's return to the lessons and forms of local architecture, which seems based on Rossi's formulation of the idea of typology that focused as much on significant parts of buildings as on whole structures, later allowed him to synthesise a new architectural language. His later work is more classical, but what passes for classical elsewhere is perhaps also vernacular in a region where the great cities of Italy are near neighbours. There were other architects working in Ticino in the 1970s who began to reconsider the canonical historic architecture of northern Italy, in particular the work of Andrea Palladio.

In Britain Palladianism is a sort of cypher for the old glories of the Country House, but in Ticino in the 1970s Palladio's work was reinterpreted as an alternative treatment of space compared to the well-worn formula of open planning. This was first seen at the Casa Tonini (1972–4) by Bruno Reichlin and Fabio Reinhart in the small suburban village of Torricella. They described it as a deliberately ironic and offensive reaction to '. . . the disparate conditions of this neighbourhood of one family homes [through] the assertion of geometry. The house programmatically confronts the real conditions of Ticino suburbia with the mathematics of the ideal villa.'[5] Ironically, it is now surrounded by the bland bungaloid developments that its architects despised.

The form of the house is based on Palladio's Villa Almerico-Valmarana (La Rotonda) of 1565–9. Made from plain concrete finely moulded, the exterior is very self-effacing despite the full-height, double-width windows at the centre of each facade and the slim, full-height windows that dematerialise the corners of the structure. It is simultaneously Modern and Palladian, and, although small, like Palladio's own buildings it has a presence beyond its size. The cruciform open plan of the ground floor rises through the whole height of the building at the central axis – an early deployment of that Post-Modern cliché the atrium, except that here it is used to reconfigure the idea of the open plan to include the vertical axis. At the centre of this space is the dining area, challenging the conventional informality of the surrounding modern suburbs by reasserting the formality of dinner.

Villa Emo, Fanzolo di Vedelago, Italy. From the 1950s onwards the architectural community made links between the works of Andrea Palladio and contemporary architectural theory. It was not until the 1970s, however, that Palladio's work – including Villa Emo (1559-65) – began to directly influence contemporary architectural practice

The revival of interest in Classicism during the 1970s was in part a result of new problems facing domestic design that were the result of new ways of living. The Modernist house of the 1950s and 1960s evolved in a period before the proliferation of white and electronic goods. By the 1970s this was beginning to change as were people's attitudes to living arrangements. Where one bath was formerly sufficient, more were now desirable. Where once bedrooms were for sleeping in, it was now recognised that they were a more complex private space; often an en-suite bathroom might be required even for children. Cars needed garages and more cars needed bigger garages. Kitchen equipment proliferated – fridges, freezers, dishwashers, double ovens, washing machines and coffee makers all required space. What re-emerged with these developments was an increasing need for separation of service spaces and living spaces that ran against the flow of Modernist house planning. By contrast, houses in the Classical tradition were designed to accommodate just such a separation of functions and included space for suites of private rooms. It is this practicality of the classical plan, rather than decorative Historicism or cultural conservatism to a consumerised household that caused architects like Mario Campi, Franco Pessina and Niki Piazzoli to re-explore Renaissance domestic design in buildings like the Casa Felder. In

House on Pucklerstrasse, Berlin, Germany.
Designed by Arno Bonovini, Klaus Lattermann and Knut Stützel, this single family house in a street of diplomats' houses in the wealthy Berlin suburb of Dahlem shows the influence of the Ticinese and Italian reassessment of Classicism. Though related to the Tonini House, it is a far looser interpretation of the proportions of the Palladian villa and also shows some influence from the local preference for houses with few windows on the street facade. The formality of the design is emphasised by the repetition of squares throughout the design and the controlled palette of white, black and grey relieved by carefully shaped greenery.

designing a modern house based on historical precedents there is no doubt that Rossi's ahistorical notion of typology could be helpful, since it defined type without the connoisseur's notion of provenance. Thus, at the Casa Felder the architects were able to deploy seemingly arcane features like porticoes and enfilades, not to mention rooms next to each other on two floors that are for the use of the maid – comprising scullery, utility room, laundry and a workroom that doubled as her private room – freed from their historical details as essences of types of design solution.

Historicism in the 1970s did not have the cultural baggage that it has now acquired. In a sense its re-examination was part of the spirit of experimentation and cultural relativism generated by the liberal culture of the 1960s. Its chief uses were a way out of the orthodoxies of Modernism towards a broader future practice. As Michael Manser has said the architects of the 1950s generation were unable to adapt to a new world and so they stuck rigidly to the Modernist dogma. New generations of architects who emerged in the countercultural atmosphere of the 1960s, not to mention the rapidly expanding consumer economy, needed new sources of ideas to deal with a more demanding, fashion-conscious clientele and new ways of thinking of space that could deal with the richer material world. The past was an obvious place to start looking.

1   Essex County Council, *Essex Design Guide for Residential Areas*, Anchor Press (Chatham), 1973.
2   Aldo Rossi, *The Architecture of the City* (1966). First published in English by MIT Press (Cambridge, MA), 1982.
3   Robert Venturi, *Complexity and Contradiction in Architecture*, MoMA Papers on Architecture, MoMA (New York), 1966.
4   Tita Carloni, 'Architecture of the Wall and not the Trilith, Building in Mario Botta' *Lotus International,* No 37, 1983, p 35. Quoted in Gerardo Brown-Manrique, *The Ticino Guide*, Princeton Architectural Press (Princeton), 1989, p 18.
5   Claude Lichtenstein, *Swiss Furniture and Interiors 1900–2000*, Arthur Ruegg (ed), Birkhauser Verlag (Basel), 2002, p 324.

Casa Bianchi

Mario Botta

Riva San Vitale, Ticino, Switzerland   1971-73

The Casa Bianchi is set in a large informal garden on the slopes of Monte San Giorgio on the outskirts of the ancient town of Riva San Vitale, which contains a basilica that dates from the 6th century. It overlooks Lake Lugano and faces Monte Generoso. The house was built for its owners, an academic and his partner whose family have lived in Riva San Vitale since the 18th century – indeed it contains many examples of furniture owned by the family for 200 years. The building recalls the form of pre-industrial vernacular tower houses in nearby villages like Rovio. Essentially it consists of four levels joined by a narrow turning stairwell entered at the upper level via a long metal bridge.

A particular feature of the tower houses is a roofed belvedere on the top floor, an essentially open space developed to cope with the combination of a hot and wet climate. This vernacular reference is challenged by the Adhocist use of cheap, commercially available construction blocks on the exterior, and the combination of these materials and the tower form gives the house a military quality. This impression is wholly misleading – in its present state the Casa Bianchi seems far more humanist than martial. The mature planting around the tower reduces its apparent scale and the interior design of the house creates the sense that the outer shell is a sheltering structure rather than a defensive one.

The living areas of the house are effectively diagonally bisected by the huge light well that drops the full height of the building at the front of the house and, to the rear, a smaller light well of the same height. These features and the various balconies arranged with different aspects on the three upper floors give the sense that the house exists within another more open structure of semi-exterior levels and spaces. On each floor rooms extend through fenestration onto room-sized balconies with commanding views of Lake Lugano, and because of the overarching exterior structure these exteriors are sheltered from the extremes of the weather. The combination of the spaces gives the sense that, far from being an enclosure, the building is in fact a very open, almost breathing, environment.

This is echoed by the open structure of the entrance bridge, almost a folly in itself, which enters the building on the third-floor balcony and thence gives

Casa Bianchi, Ticino, Switzerland. Although from the entrance side the Casa Bianchi has a formidable appearance this is to retain the privacy of the house, which is set close to an overlooking road. The other elevations are similarly discreet. However, the main purpose of the outer shell – which recalls the tower houses found in nearby villages – is to act as a shelter so that the balconies on each floor are isolated from wind and rain, but open to the sun and the warmth of the mild but damp local climate. Over the years lush planting has relieved the martial starkness that the site possessed when the house was first built.

Casa Bianchi, Ticino, Switzerland. A traditionally Modernist feature of the house is its very high living space and minimal visual separation from the exterior patio. The role of the exterior of the building as protective but open is clear from the way that the ground-floor patio space falls within the building and the upper patios overlook the lowest patio. This creation of semi-internal spaces is one of the most attractive features of this house combining in a very gentle way protection from, and pleasure in, the changing weather.

directly onto the stairs. The stairs and the apertures of the rooms that they lead onto are handled in a very idiosyncratic manner that owes more to De Stijl diagrams than anything else. The stairs are made of concrete slabs bounded by steel frames. They have no risers and are therefore open, and are flanked by similarly open-feeling vertical slabs to the centre of the well. The colour scheme here is black edging with primary colours in contrast to the overall grey of bare concrete and white-painted walls.

The doors to rooms are only about 1.5 metres in height and resemble the primary-coloured stall doors found in schools. However, here they emphasise the openness of the home and prevent the modest rooms feeling cell-like. The strong primary colours used at the Casa Bianchi date from a time when strong earth-hued browns, oranges, yellows and greens dominated the palettes of architects. Botta's use of Mondrianesque primaries, particularly yellows and blues, is far ahead of that of most of his contemporaries, who were very subdued in their use of colour, and anticipates the Lego palette of colours that characterised the Post-Modern architecture of the early 1980s.

The spaces within the house are very interesting because, unlike many Modernist designers, Botta does not focus only on large spaces. Big spaces do exist on the ground floor, where the living, kitchen and dining areas flow one into another, and space is emphasised by the way that the balcony area of the ground floor is roofed over four floors above. But as well as these spacious areas there are small, intimate, private spaces like the bathrooms, which use strong yellows and blues to, somehow, create a sense of warmth. The most attractive of these small spaces is the fireplace – practically an inglenook – at the rear of the ground floor. This is set at 45 degrees to a glazed

door that opens onto the rear garden area, which also feels enclosed because the rear of the building is built close to the gradient of the hill behind. It is possible to sit by the fireplace at a low level and look out of the 'back door', and the sense created by this is both intimate and childlike. The large size of the hearth and the polished ochre plaster of the chimney breast are reassuringly traditional in feeling, making this part of the house seem timeless and old as much as the rest seems timelessly contemporary.

Rather than displaying wear and tear after 30 years of continuous occupation, the house has developed a patina. It is a complex and labyrinthine space despite its small scale. Botta's Casa Bianchi is a very complex synthesis of ideas, effortlessly delivered with style and restraint. The challenging form of the outer shell contrasts sharply with the evident liveability of the house. Its seeming toughness contrasts with the constant pleasure of the interlinked interior and semi-exterior spaces, which maximise the possibilities of experiencing Ticino's mild climate. A rigorous contemporaneity of form and material is always leavened by intimate spaces, warm colours and a real understanding of the pleasures of a home – big meals, staring out at a view, listening to rain or huddling around a fire. What at first seems a bit of architectural vanity given form turns out to be a house that is evidently a pleasure to live in.

Above: **Casa Bianchi, Ticino, Switzerland.** At the rear of the living room is a Modern version of the inglenook fireplace. The use of soft-textured polished plaster, the cramped setting by a large, opening picture window and the provision of low sitting areas transform what could have been a 'poky' space into a warm fireside from which to watch the pleasing inaction of the garden.

Left and opposite: **Casa Bianchi, Ticino, Switzerland.** There are two colour codes that operate throughout the house. The walls, floor and ceilings of the rooms are usually in muted tones – grey ceiling, white walls, terracotta floor – and this goes well with the subtle lighting effects created by the sheltering superstructure. The built-in furnishings, the furniture and certain key-note areas – notably the bathrooms and the fireplace – utilise a different palette of strong primaries that act as highlights to the main structure. An exception is the more populated dining-kitchen area, where the movement of people performs the same moderating function on the general diffused light and muted tones.

Perlbinder House

Norman Jaffe

Sagaponack, Long Island, New York, USA   1972

On the edge of the Hamptons, in a part of Long Island that still seems remote, and lying off Sagaponack Main Street between Peters Pond and Wainscott Pond is Potato Road, the setting of Norman Jaffe's house for Steve Perlbinder. The location feels a long way from everywhere and the house is set right on the dunes above the beach. Jaffe, who set up a practice in Bridgehampton, Long Island, in 1973, was a flamboyant and domineering architect who was famous for his outspoken opinions on the subject of his clients' former homes. He built about 50 houses on Long Island in a style that was not only ostentatious in its scale and geometry, but also respectful of local history and the environment. This paradoxical combination was achieved precisely because of his exaggeration of the mundane. Unlike many Long Island architects of the time, he avoided the conceptual architecture of the New York Five and in its place took the local vernacular and the landscape as his starting point. He spoke of the need to pay 'tribute' to the surrounding landscape and, despite their flamboyance, his houses respond to local materials and the contours of their sites in a manner that reveals his interest in Frank Lloyd Wright. Ironically, he drowned swimming off Long Island in 1993.

In the early settlements on Long Island the houses were built in what is termed the salt-box style that dominated the north-east coastal regions of America. The term alludes both to their shape – like the old, lidded, wooden kitchen 'salts' – and their size. These houses were built from the local timber of the pine barrens, the small-section wooden frames being faced with boards or wooden shingles and roofed with shingles. They were often founded on fieldstones, which in the absence of brick also served as material for the chimneys. The salt box was a simple, durable and flexible way of building, easy to expand and repair, and on the East Coast it symbolises heritage as much as thatch does in Britain. In keeping with the marked nostalgia, not least for simple natural textures, of the early 1970s the Perlbinder House uses the shingle style with its simple geometry, rich surfaces and small apertures.

Jaffe's version of the style, though, is on a glamorous scale, although when it was built the *Architectural Record* thought it 'relatively smal'. Viewed close to, it is big but the lack of referents, other than the sea and the dunes, renders this gigantism imperceptible so that from a distance the house appears as a simple dark form against the pale dunes. Part of its effect derives from the use of shingles to cover the entire surface and the recessing of the windows, both of which serve to emphasise the light-absorbing blackness of the building in contrast to the intense clarity of the marine light. This sculptural simplicity is particularly strong on the land side of the house, while on the sea side the effect is more gently modulated through the use of

Perlbinder House, Long Island, USA. The main body of the building is in the form of a traditional salt-box house. This origin is very clear on the land side *(see page 220),* where the few windows and completely shingled surface echo the spartan living conditions in the fishing villages of north-eastern America, though on a palatial scale. Seen from the ocean, the right side of the building shows the almost immaterial glass box that joins the kitchen–dining area to the owners' suite in the new extension. The old master bedroom is indicated by the balcony cut into the roof above the large windows of the kitchen–dining area, with the left half of the building given over to the living areas.

Opposite and right: **Perlbinder House, Long Island, USA.** As well as being open across the entire plan of the house and to the eaves for much of its area, the living space is also cunningly split, with the larger 'guest area' situated below the more private upper, owners' living area, which can only be accessed by passing through the kitchen to the upper landing that also accesses the old master bedroom. This area receives its own light from the ocean-facing skylight above.

Above: **Perlbinder House, Long Island, USA.** Sabellarosa has joined the old with the new by continuing the full-height windows of the dining area of the Jaffe house out of the old building and around 360 degrees to encompass a lobby leading to stairs down to the owners' suite of rooms. Though the new work is clearly indicated by a change in timber and lighter structural elements, Sabellarosa has retained the tone of the Jaffe woodwork, while paying homage to his predecessor's work and expressing his difference from it by using a glass wall to separate the old exterior from the new extension, where a lesser architect would simply have used the old exterior wall as a new interior surface.

large picture windows framing an abstractly treated rough-stone fire wall and bronze patinated chimney stack, and the family swimming pool that lies between the house and the sea.

Originally the house had a suite of rooms for the children, including their own entrance, on the ground level, a guest suite facing inland above this and a master suite facing the sea. Since then the owners have had to deal with a fire and the imminent destruction of the house by the sea, the currents of which have scoured away the beach on which the building stands. The family has also grown up and the children now have children. Other people might have moved but the Perlbinders decided to move the house. At the same time, it was decided to bring it up to date by the addition of new private rooms designed by the Brazilian architect Cristian Sabellarosa.

The house was originally built on the back of a sand dune on deep piles, and before moving it to its new position 300 feet inland from the original site a new dune had to be built. The house was lifted by a crane and placed on more robust foundations as the new plan involved developing a much larger ground floor than in the original residence. In the new design the east and west ends of the house were to be extended to provide more modern accommodation for the Perlbinders and the families of their children. It was decided that these new extensions would be single storey and thus extend either side of what was effectively the basement level of the old house. This had views inland but not towards the sea as it sat below the level of the dune. The new extensions are also for the most part below dune level and their roofs form an extended patio area for the sea side of the old house, except at the eastern end where the new extension extends beyond the dune to provide views towards the sea. Between the house and the sea is a swimming pool nestling in the dunes.

The new extension addresses some of the problems of the old 1970s building, and by doing so emphasises the principal qualities that it possesses. In common with most houses of the period the original Jaffe design treated the bedroom and bath areas as essentially service rooms subservient to the

main drama of the design. Although there were three bathrooms and three distinct areas of bedrooms and studies in the old design, these were rather small and spartan. The bathrooms, in particular, were treated as places of ablution rather than as places of leisure and relaxation. In the new extension the atmosphere is very different. There are more bedrooms, each with its own individual character reflecting the desires of the owner, as do the large *en-suite* bathrooms. The new, more sybaritic, mood is represented in one bathroom, which has a polished concrete bath that can constantly overflow into runnels that carry the water away under a glass floor. There is also a media room, which would have been beyond technical necessity in the old house.

Throughout the new extension the rooms are lit by floor-to-ceiling glazing through which light is diffused by a hardwood and polycarbonate *brise-soleil*. The overall effect is of a bright yet softly lit and very private succession of finely detailed simplicity, where the luxury of expensive timber and steel is leavened by the use of polished concrete and the beautifully plain exposed concrete of the retaining wall. If the new extension brings a contemporary sense of luxury to the house, the original Jaffe interior offers spectacular space grand enough for entertaining on a lavish scale.

Jaffe's design combined the basic division of domestic space into a large living–eating area surrounded by much smaller rooms – a Modernist fundamental – with the New York Five approach to interiors that favoured creating a continuous circulation space that rises through levels given over to different functions. What is unique about Jaffe's use of these ideas is the drama that he is able to generate from them. In essence, the majority of the interior of the salt-box shell is given over to a single space that rises from the lowest level of the house right up to the eaves. Within this space the floor rises through a spiral of broad, open levels linked by shallow stairs so that a feeling of the height of the ceiling is maintained, despite the fact that the last levels of the dining and cooking area have a low ceiling because they sit beneath the master bedroom, which occupies the upper reaches of the east end of the room.

The sense of height is preserved because one is always aware of the proximity of large space, an effect created by way that the upper levels look down into space as well as up. Being in the interior feels like being in a large

medieval hall full of 20th-century technology, and this effect is created in part
by the use of materials. The whole space is lined with cedar siding and floored
with black slate. The intelligent device of having a large dining table and the
work surfaces in the kitchen area in the same slate as the floor is used to
create a strange continuum where the table and the kitchen unit–sideboard
appear to morph into the floor of the level above.

A key element in this transition is the dramatic and unexpected feature
that the edge of the upper kitchen level is formed by a solid-wood-faced
range of units into which are set the sinks. These, then, are in fact in the floor
of this upper level. This whole arrangement turns the kitchen into a kind of
theatre with its own stalls and circle. Equally interesting is the siting of the
large range in an east-facing bay, which is both practical for the cook and
takes the cooking away from the preparation and serving area, thus removing
the messiest part of preparing food from the drama of its observation.

The progression through the hall to the inner sanctum of the dining area
is equally theatrical. One enters the house at the lowest level in a low-
ceilinged lobby, which then leads into a sudden increase in light and height
as a short return, lit by a large square window set low, leads up into a void
that goes right up to the eaves. Although one can see the height of the space
as one rises, a parapet prevents one from seeing the floor area until the last
minute. This space runs the full width of the building and rises up its full
height, and is lit by picture window leading to a patio and an uninterrupted
view of the ocean.

On the far side next to the patio window is an open fire set in a rough
stone wall. To its left is a short rise to the dining area, with its own large
window and ocean view, and then another to the back of the kitchen area.
This leads, past stairs to the master bedroom, to a sort of balcony that stands
high above the entrance stairs so that the owners can stand here and look
down on guests arriving. To reach the furthest level, which paradoxically lies
just above the entry, the layout makes it necessary to walk the full length of
the perimeter of the salt box adding to the sense of size. The effect of the
whole is regal in its impression because of a combination of the increasingly
personal spaces, which are always visible from the grand public spaces, and
the sense that one is progressing towards these ever more intimate areas.

Johnston House

David Johnston CBE

Longburgh, Burgh by Sands, Cumbria, UK   1976

Longburgh is typical of many north British farming settlements. It is a street village of substantial farmhouses and, close by, farm buildings built on land that rises out of the low-lying meadows of the Eden estuary near where the river falls into the Solway Firth. Overlooked by the cloud-shouldering Pennines, it is a landscape of green pasture rimmed with hedges punctuated by ash trees and narrow roads leading to salt marshes under a wide, iron-grey sky. The light and the weather are hard, and the farmhouses have a regular solidity that is redolent of protection and durability. This type of building isn't really architecture nor is it vernacular in the sense of thatched cottages since most of the buildings in these settlements date from the late 18th to the mid 19th century. They are examples of utilitarian building in its most developed form, made from excellent materials worked by the most professional of craftsmen. Their attraction lies in this hard-hatted correctness, in their large ungenerous exteriors that somehow suggest a warmer interior. They are the architectural equivalent of a good mahogany chair.

It would be entirely appropriate for the architect David Johnston – who made his career as a consultant architect to many public projects in Cumbria – to live in one of these houses, which serve equally as well as a rectory or lawyer's house as a farmhouse, and can be seen as monuments to the ascendancy of the professional middle class. Instead he decided to build one of his own.

Throughout the 1970s there had been an increasing interest in vernacular architecture and a corresponding decrease in interest in Modernism, to the extent that in 1973 Essex County Council produced the *Essex Design Guide for Residential Areas* for public and private developments alike. The legacy of this apparently humanistic intervention against the forces of mass-housing Modernism has been the proliferation of tiny-roomed East Anglian houses across the whole of Britain. Recently, with the revival in interest in Modernism, it is Historicism that has been attacked. David Johnston's design for his own house is a rare example of the vernacular and Modernist traditions living happily side by side, combining, as it does, the sensible architecture developed in the region to deal with the vagarious local weather and the advances in indoor living conditions represented by Modernism.

The exterior appearance of the Johnston House is barely distinguishable from that of its neighbours except when a close inspection reveals modern materials and technologies. Notwithstanding the use of modern double-glazing that combines a system produced in the North with concrete window frames instead of ones in sandstone, the house was built by a local firm that had been building this type of house since the early 19th century. The

Above: **Johnston House, Cumbria, UK.** The front door shows the effect of older proportions on lowering the apparent height of the ceiling, while on the other hand being constructed in a very British Modernism of flush solid oak set with stainless-steel ironmongery.

Right: **Johnston House, Cumbria, UK.** The house combines the utilitarian solidity of the northern middle-class home of the late 18th or early 19th century with the plan of a modern house. Taken from Arts and Crafts precedents, the plan places the kitchen, stairs, landing, study and smaller bedrooms to the front of the house. At the rear, the ground floor is almost entirely given over to an open-plan living area, increased in size by an extension into the large garden. The construction and proportions continue the theme of combining new ideas and vernacular traditions – the white-painted brick, concrete door frames and window surrounds, and the wooden-framed double-glazed windows. The roof is traditional slate and the proportions replicate those used locally in the late 18th century

standard of construction is immaculate. It reflects a Modernist regard for detail in the architect and a similar perfectionism in the builder, and is so high that the exterior brick surface would serve equally as well as an unadorned interior wall – every brick is true and level with its neighbours and the mortar between them never varies in width or surface finish. However, what really distinguishes the Johnston House is not simply that it is well built but that it is correctly proportioned. In any age of building there are standard proportions of rooms, windows, doors, stairs and so on, and in Britain, particularly since the Second World War, these have become taller and

Johnston House, Cumbria, UK. The living area shows a Modernist use of exposed brick, big windows, white paint, Berber carpet, translucent floor-to-ceiling 'slubby' curtains, standard lamp, Japanese light shade and a Baxi fire. The combination of a country Sheraton dining suite, a Regency piano and other antiques from various periods shows the British appreciation of the common spirit of design between pre-Victorian crafts and post-Victorian Modernism, which finds an analogue in the exterior combination of vernacular and modern elements.

Johnston House, Cumbria, UK. Pre-industrial levels of detailing and craft have ensured that the bathroom and kitchen, which are commonly regarded as having a limited life span, have remained unchanged for 30 years. An admiration for the durability of vernacular forms is inherent in the attention to detail apparent in the immaculate tile- and brickwork. The simple purity of the modern sinks and basin has been carefully selected with the same fastidiousness shown in the owners' love of uncomplicated Georgian furniture.

thinner whereas the proportions of the old local buildings nearby were lower and fatter, less oblong and more square. Johnston has used this proportioning throughout the house. It is for this reason as much as any other that it looks correct in its context, and is free of the awkward gestural Historicism of many subsequent backward-looking buildings built in the name of contextual harmony.

Inside, the old proportions are less apparent because of the thoroughgoing Modernism of the interior. But here too the older form works well with what, after decades of Modernism, is also a kind of vernacular. The layout of the house conforms to some very old ideas, with five good-sized bedrooms and a bathroom all entered from a central landing accessed from below by stairs that turn on a half-landing. Downstairs there are, as might be expected, a study, a kitchen with a scullery and, beyond, a storage room and garage. But the essence of the modernity of the house lies in the fact that about two-thirds of the ground floor is an open-planned living area well lit by large windows with a double aspect and long views. Equally from the British domestic Modernist tradition is the white paint on every wall, except one of exposed brick that surrounds a Baxi coal fire set below a flush-fitting stone lintel. The kitchen, bathroom and other service areas of the house use modern technologies and materials with an almost Swiss discretion and precision, so that in the kitchen the teak draining board and worktop have no trace of their 30 years of family use. The unique quality of this house is its timelessness and the uncanny feeling that it is a proper grown-up home. If an early 19th-century builder could build the best house he could now he would have done it like this. The house is neither new nor old, but would be part of a continuum if there were many other buildings of the same standard.

Casa Felder

Mario Campi, Franco Pessina and Niki Piazzoli
Lugano, Ticino, Switzerland   1978-80

Casa Felder sits in the tranquil isolation of the family estate close to the centre of Lugano, its splendid view of the sugar loaf mountain disturbed only by the huge spurt of water that erupts from a fountain by the lake below. The estate is remarkable in that, sited in the fruit gardens and vineyards surrounding the original 18th-century Villa, are two modern houses built for successive female generations. Campi, Pessina and Piazzoli's Casa Felder was built on the occasion of the marriage of the daughter of the owners of the old house, and the latest villa on the estate was built for the daughter of the owner of Casa Felder. Were this a Victorian novel nothing would seem unusual, but in our own time the commissioning of successive and assertively contemporary houses proximate to the historic family home shows an uncommon commitment to the contemporary.

Such a commission also presented the architects with an unusual challenge: to design a new home suitable for the restrained and timeless aura of the old house and its agricultural gardens. A further consideration in the case of the Casa Felder was that their client required only three bedrooms, yet the site requires a building with considerable presence. Casa Felder was Campi Pessina and Piazzoli's first house and it displays a typology that has become a hallmark of the partnership's, and later Campi's, domestic work. The form of the house is almost four cubes, made up of three ranges around a courtyard and terminated on the fourth side by a row of columns linked by a pediment.

The overt Palladianism of the form and scale of the villa is echoed in the classical orientation. The public approach to the villa is obscured by greenery that only reveals a double-height entry that gives little clue as to the scale of the house. The range with the commanding view of the lake houses a large living room beneath a very traditional enfilade of rooms above for the owners. Leading from the atrium hall, a study gives way to a bathroom, dressing room, bedroom and finally a balcony in a succession of increasingly private spaces. The range at the back of the courtyard, which has the least interesting outward aspect, contains a double-height atrium that gives onto the kitchen and related service rooms on the ground floor, and above that a series of service rooms for the laundry and linen of the house.

The atrium is terminated at one end by the entrance to the house with its double-height glazing and at the other by a dining room on the ground floor with a study above. Access to the upper part of the house is by small 'service' stairs by the entrance and grander, more dramatic, main stairs linking the primary private rooms with the dining and living rooms below. The final range

Below: **Casa Felder, Ticino, Switzerland.** The architects have achieved many trompe l'oeils with this house. From the road entrance to the estate, the building is only apparent as a door set at the end of an avenue of bay and box. On the garden side the porticoed wall gives the strong impression of a Palladian villa, while in fact screening the courtyard of a three-sided house.

Above: **Casa Felder, Ticino, Switzerland.** These trompe l'oeil devices combine traditional signifiers of grandeur – the avenue and the portico – with late Modern Neoclassicism, grid-like design and flat, white forms to create a contemporary home that has elegant gravitas but not size.

Right and below: **Casa Felder, Ticino,
Switzerland.** Together with the courtyard, the
atrium is the public space in the house; it even
has a vestigial balcony overlooking the courtyard
from the top of the principal stairs. These connect
the main living and dining areas on the ground
floor with the master suite above, while a smaller
spiral stair at the far end of the entrance hall leads
discreetly to the service rooms situated off the
upper levels of the atrium and to the
children's–guest wing.

Opposite: **Casa Felder, Ticino, Switzerland.** The
house is made up of two residential wings separated by an atrium behind which lie service rooms.
The wings are united by the courtyard, which the
atrium and master wing overlook through full-height
windows that can be opened to extend the inner
space into the courtyard and vice versa. The atrium is glazed in with a small grid of lights on the
upper level, which retains the privacy of the upper
floors while still enabling the space to be well lit,
and also creates the sense of a wall above the
apparently open lower level. As with the exterior,
the overall effect is to create the feeling of a
palazzo without the commensurate scale.

contains access to a carport sited beneath its the upper floor and other
service rooms on the ground floor, while above are two bedrooms with
adjacent bathrooms.

The Casa Felder combines Palladian aesthetics with the highly developed
hierarchy of space and function found in aristocratic homes of the turn of the
18th and 19th centuries and the simplicity of form and punctilious attention
to detail characteristic of Modernism. Nowhere is this more clearly seen than
in the contrast between the living room and the kitchen. The former
epitomises the simple luxury of open space, bounded on two sides just by
glazing, while the wall facing the entrance contains only a large fireplace. In
contrast the kitchen is almost the realisation of the term 'domestic science'.
It is large and contains the finest technology of its day, housed in unitised
storage, together with furniture specifically designed for the space. This uses
typical utilitarian materials of the period, produced to such a high standard as
to transcend the disposability that characterises the 'fitted kitchen' style.

In many ways, Casa Felder epitomises the reinvention of the villa form in the 1970s through the reappraisal of precedents in Vitruvius and Palladio that offer a formal language of spaces capable of meeting the needs of a contemporary demand for luxury. This demand is not about maximising space or the use of fine materials or providing for lots of servants; rather, it is about creating modest spaces designed to the highest standards in homes supported by a discreet and effective technical infrastructure. In the recent past domestic luxury was in part defined by large areas for public entertaining and the display of artefacts. However, in modern times and in the distant past, domestic luxury had more to do with creating convivial spaces. Some social areas are well placed for the best weather and aspect, while others maximise the satisfactions of private life – be it sleeping, bathing or contemplation.

In the Modernist house of the post-war era great attention was paid to the quality of the living and eating areas, often at the cost of sleeping and bathing, but late 1970s houses like Casa Felder show careful consideration of the more private spaces of the home through the provision of individual bathrooms, and by making sleeping and dressing areas more significant rather than simply convenient spaces. Equally, contemporary household technology had reached a level of ubiquity, efficiency and standardisation that, in a very compact area, enabled the kind of service provision previously only found in homes with many servants. At Casa Felder this allowed the architects to create a house that is small but grand at the same time. This sense of modest grandeur is in part created by the combination of a design that emulates the Palladian villa, but uses the simple surfaces and colours of the Modern Movement to rein back any sense of pomposity, while the exact attention to detailing throughout the entire house is a discreet statement of absolute quality.

Above: Casa Felder, Ticino, Switzerland.
Upstairs the rooms are arranged into a suite
that effectively makes this area a house within
a house, in which some rooms look out over
the lake and others, like the main bedroom,
look inward over the private courtyard.

Right: **Casa Felder, Ticino, Switzerland** With an
almost *ancien régime* effect, one of the wings of
the house is given over to rooms for the owners.
The ground floor has a large living room that is
terminated by an impressive open fireplace, while
the sides are dematerialised by full-height glazing.
Thus, this room is reduced to its most important
elements: a large fire, big sofas and a sense of
unrestricted space.

Further Reading

Banham, Reyner, *The Architecture of the Well-tempered Environment*, University of Chicago Press (Chicago, Il), 1969

A history of the effect on architectural design of the new technologies for controlling the internal environment of buildings through the previous 100 years.

Brown-Manrique, Gerardo, *The Ticino Guide*, Princeton Architectural Press (New York), 1989

Detailed and informative guide to architecture in Ticino with good introduction.

Conran, Terence, *The House Book*, Mitchell Beazley Publishers Ltd (London), 1974

Classic guide to middle-class taste of the 1970s in Britain.

Crompton, Dennis, Lachmayer, Herbert and Schoenig, Pasqual (eds), *A Guide to Archigram 1961–74*, Academy Editions (London), 1994

A compilation and overview of Archigram magazine from 1961 to 1974. There is a companion volume of essays about Archigram.

Daguerre, Mercedes, with an essay by Roman Hollenstein, *Birkhauser Architectural Guide, Switzerland: 20th Century*, Birkhauser Verlag (Basel), 1997.

Good basic gazetteer of Swiss Modernism.

Disch, Peter, *50 Anni di Architettura in Ticino 1930–1980*, Quaderno della Rivista Tecnica della Svizzera Italiana, Grassico Publicita SA (Belinzona-Lugano), 1983

Very thorough gazetteer of Ticino Modernism with more listings than either of the guides listed above.

Dobney, Stephen (ed), *Alfredo De Vido: Selected and Current Works*, The Master Architect Series III, Images Publishing (Mulgrave, Victoria), 1998

A good survey of the work of this able and flexible architect.

Einzig, Richard, *Classic Modern Houses in Europe*, Nichols Publishing Co (London), 1982

Rare and attractive compilation of photographs by an excellent architectural photographer.

Fiell, Charlotte and Peter (eds), *70s Decorative Art: A Source Book*, Benedikt Taschen Verlag GmbH (Cologne), 2000

A compilation of features from the Decorative Art Yearbooks of the 1970s that gives a very good worldwide sampling of the domestic architecture of the decade.

Frampton, Kenneth, 'Towards a critical regionalism: Six points for an architecture of resistance' in Hal Foster (ed), *The Anti-Aesthetic*, Bay Press (Port Townsend, WA), 1983

Critique of the globalising tendencies of Modernist architecture.

Graham, Alastair, *Romantic Modernist: The Life and Work of Norman Jaffe*, Monacelli Press (New York), 2005

A new book concentrating on Jaffe who was a prolific architect on Long Island from the 1970s until his death.

Gordon, Alastair, *Weekend Utopia: Modern Living in the Hamptons*, Princeton Architectural Press, (New York), 2001.

This is good account of the development of Modernism on Long Island in the late 20th century.

Jacobs, Jane, *The Death and Life of Great American Cities*, Vintage Books (New York), 1961

The first significant sustained argument against the Modernist doctrines of urban renewal that were prevalent in the 1940s and 1950s.

Jencks, Charles, *Modern Movements in Architecture*, Penguin Books Ltd (Harmondsworth), 1973

Good survey of the Modern Movement written before he became committed to Post-Modernism.

Jencks, Charles, *The Language of Post-Modern Architecture*, Academy Editions (London), 197.

A seminal text of Post-Modern architecture though in fact a development of positions already evident in *Modern Movements in Architecture*.

Lang, Peter and Menking,William, *Superstudio: A Life Without Objects*, Skira Editore (Milan), 2003

An account of the genesis and activities of Superstudio, in part by the protagonists themselves, but doesn't concern itself with their architectural output.

Rave, Rolf, Knofel, Hans-Joachim and Rave, Jan, *Bauen Der 70er Jahre In Berlin*, Verlag Kiepert (Berlin), 1981

Fantastic guide with good clear map and plans but short descriptions – there is a good companion book covering the building in Berlin since 1900

Robinson, John Martin, *The Latest Country Houses*, The Bodley Head (London), 1984

Features some very good Modernist country houses though in general the text favours the revivalist styles emerging at the time when it was written.

Rossi, Aldo, *The Architecture of the City*, MIT Press (Cambridge, MA), 1982

Important repositioning of the study and significance for Modern architecture of urbanism. Influential on Post-Modern architects and architects of La Tendenza.

Rowe, Colin, *Mathematics of the Ideal Villa and Other Essays*, MIT Press (Cambridge, MA), 1977

Collection featuring his famous essay on Renaissance villas, which was influential on the post-war generation of Modernist architects in Britain, America and Italy.

Ruegg, Arthur (ed), *Swiss Furniture and Interiors 1900–2000*, Birkhauser Verlag (Basel), 2002

Good account of Swiss interior and furniture design but needs to be combined with one of the guides listed above.

Tombazis, Alexandros N, *Tombazis and Associates Architects: Less is Beautiful*, L'Arca Edizione Spa (Milan), 2002

Useful non-analytic survey of many Tombazis' buildings – Tombazis Associates have also published a book featuring details of early domestic projects available from the offices of Tombazis Associates.

Venturi, Robert, *Complexity and Contradiction in Architecture*, MoMA Papers on Architecture, MoMA (New York), 1966

Influential reassessment of Baroque/Mannerist architecture that is also an attack on simplistic Modernist architecture.

Venturi, Robert, Scott-Brown, Denise and Izenour, Steven, *Learning from Las Vegas*, MIT Press (Cambridge, MA), 1972

A book in praise of the richness of popular architecture and also a plea for more meaningful architecture – pro-Modern but anti-Modernist.

Worner, Martin, Mollen Schott, Doris and Huter, Karl-Heinz, *Architekturfuhrer Berlin*, Dietrich Reimer Verlag (Berlin), 1989

Excellent gazetteer of Berlin architecture with good detail on each listed building and a good introduction.

The Architects

Mario Botta (b 1943) was born in Mendrisio, in the Ticino, the Italian-speaking canton in southern Switzerland. He studied at the Liceo Artistico in Milan and the Instituto Universitario di Architecturra in Venice. He gained early experience with Ticinese architect Tita Carloni, then, later worked as an assistant to Le Corbusier and Louis Kahn. He established his own practice in Lugano, Switzerland in 1969 and established his international reputation with the Casa Bianchi at Riva San Vitale, Ticino (1971–3), followed by the Casa Bianchi at Ligornetto, Ticino (1975) and the Casa Rotondo, Stabia (1980–2). Other buildings from his large oeuvre include the Gothard Bank, Lugano (1982–8) and the Museum of Modern Art, San Francisco, (1989–5), the Cathedral at Evry, France (1995) and the Chapel at Monte Tamaro, Rivera, Ticino (1996). *www.botta.ch*

In 1960 **Mario Campi** (b 1936) graduated in architecture from ETH Zurich, where he later taught from 1985 to 1990. In 1961 he and **Franco Pessina** set up in partnership in Lugano; in 1969 they were joined by **Niki Piazzoli**. The firm won international recognition for its designs for private houses and the restoration of Belinzona's Castello Montebello (1974). From 1975 Campi also began to develop the teaching side of his career and in 1985 became a professor at ETH in Zurich. As well as being a very successful commercial architect for clients that include IBM and ETH, he has also won acclaim for social projects such as the subsidised housing in the Via Beltramina, Lugano (1992). Since 1997 Campi has headed his own practice; in 2001 he won the competition for the Europark at the Eurogate urban development project in Zurich.

Christopher Day was born in Wales where he lives today. He is a graduate of the Architectural Association with a longstanding commitment to Green issues, expressed in his book, *Places of the Soul: Architecture and Environmental Design as a Healing Art*, HarperCollins, 1990. He is a teacher as well as an architect. His major work is around his home Pen-y Lyn, which he has been developing since 1975.

Alfredo De Vido (b 1932) graduated as a Master of Fine Arts in Architecture from Princeton in 1956. He then served in the 'Seabees' (the US Navy's Construction Battallions), and during this time built a number of houses in Japan at Atsugi, for which he was commended by the regional Japanese government. He subsequently attended the Royal Academy of Fine Arts in Copenhagen, gaining a diploma in Town Planning. During the 1960s, he worked in Italy in the offices of The Architects Collaborative and for Marcel Breuer in the USA. In 1968 he set up his own practice in New York. A prolific architect with a large domestic practice output, he has designed a number of homes that have been *Architectural Record* houses. He has developed modular building systems as an aid to design innovation and construction in domestic architecture. *www.devido.architects.com*

Gian Piero Frassinelli (b 1939) trained as an architect at the Florence School of Architecture, where he actively participated in the student movement. He graduated in 1968 while the school was occupied by students. His interest in architecture was tempered by an interest in anthropology and politics. He joined the Superstudio group in 1968 and later became their archivist. From the early 1970s he became interested in the demotic architecture and building methods of Italy. Much of his freelance work has been involved in the restoration of old buildings, as well as some social housing projects.

Dieter Frowein (b 1938) is a Berlin-based architect and author who worked with Jurgen Sawade on a number of projects, including the Neumann Haus at Scharfe Lanke and a Seniorenwohnhaus on Schlossstrasse, Charlottenburg, Berlin (1976–78). In partnership with Gerhard Spangenberg, he has also worked on the Kirche St Jacobi, Oranienstrasse in Kreuzberg, Berlin (1979–82), where they added two new priest houses, and more recently on a housing block at the Wohnpark am Berlin Museum, Lindenstrasse (1984–86), a mixed restoration and urban redevelopment project. **Jurgen Sawade** (b 1937) was a pupil and former assistant of O M Ungers. In the late 1970s, he began to specialise in large-scale buildings. These include a seven-storey block of four houses at Lewishamstrasse in Charlottenburg, Berlin (1979–81) and the restoration of Peter Mendelsohn's Neue Schaubuhne Theatre (1928), which he undertook between 1975 and 1981.

Wolfgang Goschel and Rosemarie Barthel were part of Architektengruppe Wassertorplatz based in Kreuzberg, Berlin. The group's most well known work is the Heiligenkreuz church on Oranienburger Strasse, Kreuzberg, Berlin.

Patrick Gwynne (1913-2003) is most well known as the architect of The Homewood, the house he built in 1937 for his parents in Esher, Surrey, now owned by the National Trust. Throughout his long career, though, he produced a number of idiosyncratic Modern buildings that include a restaurant for the Festival of Britain and one on the Serpentine (1964 and 1971), as well as houses for actors Lawrence Harvey and Jack Hawkins. He also designed a number of houses in Blackheath, London, for the property developer Leslie Bilsby, in an exuberant style quite different from Bilsby's speculative SPAN architect, Eric Lyons.

Richard Henderson (b 1928) and Charles Gwathmey formed the partnership of Gwathmey Henderson in 1966; it was dissolved in 1971 when Charles Gwathmey established the famous New York firm of Gwathmey Siegel with Robert Siegel. The years of the Gwathmey Henderson partnership were marked by the creation of widely recognised designs for houses, including the Gwathmey House at Amagansett (1965–7); the Steel House, Bridgehampton (1968–9); the Cogan House, Bridgehampton (1971–2); and the Mandel House, Huntington Bay, which was credited to Henderson when his partnership with Gwathmey ended.

Sir Michael Hopkins (b 1935) and **Patty Hopkins** (b 1942) set up in practice together in 1976, at the same time as they were creating their house in Hampstead. Michael Hopkins had earlier worked with Norman Foster. Subsequent commissions included the Greene King Brewery bottling plant at Bury St Edmunds (1981), the Mound Stand at Lord's Cricket Ground, London (1987), the new Opera House at Glyndebourne, Sussex, (1992–4), the Inland Revenue Buildings in Nottingham, (1992–4), the New Parliamentary Building, Westminster (2000), and the Wellcome Foundation, London (2005).
www.hopkins.co.uk

Norman Jaffe (1933-93) began building resort houses in Long Island in the late 1960s. In 1973 he moved his practice to Bridgehampton, Long Island, and by 1993, when he died in a swimming accident in the sea, he had built over 60 houses on Long Island, some of which are *Architectural Record* houses. These combined flamboyant Modernism with landscape and local vernacular references. His work is the subject of a new book by Alastair Graham, *Romantic Modernist: The Life and Work of Norman Jaffe*, Monacelli Press (New York) 2005.

David Johnston (b 1927) was educated at St Bees School, Cumbria. He trained at the Architectural Association and studied with Stillman and Eastwick-Field before joining the family practice, Johnston & Wright, in Carlisle, established in 1885. His particular interest and expertise is low-cost housing in the north of England, for which he was awarded an OBE in 1980.
jwarchitects.co.uk

Josef Paul Kleihues (1933-2004) studied architecture in Stuttgart, Berlin and Paris. His early work was influenced by New Brutalism and Structualism, but then, in the 1960s, he became interested in Italian Neo-Rationalism. Among architects he gained a reputation with his Workshops for the Berlin Sanitation Service, including Berlin Templehof (1969–87) and the Neukoln Hospital, Berlin, begun in 1973. He was also a teacher, writer and, between 1979 and 1983, planning director of the Berlin Internationalen Bauausstellung. Through these activities he helped shape the architecture of Berlin in the 1980s and 1990s. Latterly, he became interested in the re-use and preservation of old buildings, as in his conversion of the Hamburger Bahnhof to an art gallery between 1989 and 1996, and between 1997 and 2001 he converted a building for the Bundesministerium für Arbeit und Sozialordnung in Berlin. He was also architect of the Chicago Museum of Contemporary Art (1991–96).
www.kleihues.com

Michael Manser established The Manser Practice in 1961. He gained a reputation through his minimalist designs for steel and glass houses, including a house for himself and his family in Leatherhead, Surrey (1961), Firth House in Goldalming, Surrey (1962) and Capel Manor at Horsmonden, Kent (1970). He was awarded a CBE in 1993, was President of the Royal Institute of British Architects between 1983 and 1985, and is now Chairman of The Britannia National Homebuilders Awards and is on the awards committee of the RIBA Manser Medal. Established in 2001, the latter is awarded annually for one-off houses and presented during the RIBA Stirling Prize ceremony. He is regularly invited to act as an awards assessor and consultant for public projects, and is an Academician for both the Royal Academy of Arts and the Royal West of England Academy. As Chairman he remains a vital part of The Manser Practice, which is now managed by his son Jonathan Manser and a board of Directors.

www.manser.co.uk

Sep Marti (b 1932) trained initially in technical drawing and then, later, as an architect at ETH in Zurich, graduating in 1958. Between 1961 and 1970 he practised architecture in Arosa and Bad Ragaz in Switzerland, and then from 1973 in Zurich and Locarno. His work has been wide ranging, including factories, houses, clinics and restoration work. He is also an exhibiting artist and sculptor.

Barbara (b 1928) and **Julian Neski** (1927–2004) met while working in the New York office of J L Sert, and married in 1954. They then worked in the office of Marcel Breuer. Julian left first and, working with the architect Peter Blake, he gained his first experience of building at the east end of Long Island. The couple set up their own architectural partnership in the early 1960s. The Neski's first Long Island House was the Chalif House in East Hampton (1964), and their first prize-winning building was the Gorman House of 1968. They worked continuously as a partnership until Julian Neski's death in 2004, and over the years they built many houses on Long Island of which a number were *Architectural Record* houses.

Luigi Snozzi (b 1932) graduated in Architecture from the Federal Polytechnic of Zurich in 1957. Since then he has been both a teacher and a prolific architect. He has had two partnerships: with Livio Vacchini in Locarno, from 1962 to 1971; and Bruno Jenni in Zurich, from 1975 to 1988. Since 1988 he has worked heading his own practice in Lausanne. He is well known for his Modernist houses and for his long-term project in the village of Monte Carasso, Ticino, begun in 1977 and lasting until 1994. In 1993, he won the Prince of Wales Architecture Award.

Alexandros Tombazis (b 1939) was born in Karachi. Having graduated with honours from the Athens University School of Architecture in 1962, he subsequently acted as assistant, first to the professor of the Athens University School of Architecture and then, from 1964 to 1966, to Dr C A Doxiadis. He has had his own practice since 1963. He is external examiner in the Department of Architecture and Building Science at the University of Strathclyde, Glasgow, and a member of the American Institute of Architects. He now has a large commercial practice and clients include Procter & Gamble and Pepsico. He also specialises in environmentally friendly projects such as the new laboratories at the Centre for Renewable Energy Sources, Pikermi, Athens (1996).

www.meletitiki.gr

Alan Tye (b 1933) is a chartered architect and one of fewer than ten Royal Designers for Industry for product design. He is guest Professor of Industrial Design at The Royal Academy, Copenhagen. He has over 30 International Design Awards and holds Intellectual Property rights and patents on around 160 products, many of which have also been very successful commercially. He is best known for his Modric range of architectural ironmongery: introduced in 1965, it remains the best selling range in the world. For the last eight years Alan's studio has developed a unique design specialisation called Healthy Industrial Design (HID) and a new design methodology based on health, Sananomics. This work is particularly beneficial in the design of products in domestic and workplace environments. In July 1993 Alan Tye was presented an award by HRH Prince Philip in recognition for his studio's work in Healthy Industrial Design. The new studio for the practice of Healthy Industrial Design HID™ received a Royal Institute of British Architects Design Award in 1996.

alantyedesignstudio.co.uk